FINAL VERDICT

Judgment by Jesus Christ

Thomas D. Logie

Order this book online at www.trafford.com
or email orders@trafford.com

Most Trafford titles are also available at major online book retailers.

Printed in the United States of America.

ISBN: 978-1-4669-9333-4 (sc)
ISBN: 978-1-4669-9332-7 (e)

Trafford rev. 05/03/2013

 www.trafford.com

North America & international
toll-free: 1 888 232 4444 (USA & Canada)
phone: 250 383 6864 ♦ fax: 812 355 4082

CONTENTS

GENERAL INTRODUCTION

As I compose this in April 2013, world conditions are going from bad to worse. Adultery and other sexual acts outside marriage are commonplace. Same-sex marriage is becoming accepted from New England to New Zealand. Improvised anti-personnel weapons designed to kill are being used from Boston to Baghdad. Conflict between male and female appears to be at an all-time high, although there is no exact measure for this. Consider the ethics of many males in India that condone rape. Then contrast this with feminism in intellectual circles of the Western world. These extremes are polar opposites, but they share one characteristic—total rejection of the formation and structure of the family as taught in the Bible. Modern feminism at its core seeks to make men unnecessary even to father or raise children. By detaching men from family, modern feminism will feed its enemy, the unrestrained male. Many men, if denied reasonable hope of marriageable women, will seize some sort of sordid outlet for their libido, whether war, rape or prostitution. This can be observed in American gang culture as well as in past conduct by conquering armies throughout history.

Abortion has become a world-wide business. In America convenience of the parents and especially of the mother seems to be a prominent factor, while in Asia parents tend to murder children in the womb based on their sex. Females are undesirable because of the expensive dowries required to marry them off at the appropriate age. European and Japanese birth rates are so low that new births will not maintain the population at current levels.

When one turns to business, the moral climate does not look better. The U.S. Congress has allowed the SEC to forbid insider trading by the general public, but there has been no bar for members of Congress to use their own inside knowledge for profitable trades. Bankers around the world have aided and abetted tax evasion and helped launder drug money. At least one U.S. state government has had to accept a consent decree from the SEC for misrepresenting the finances underpinning its own state bonds. The Federal government's discussion of its own budget contains misrepresentations that would be cause for prosecution if done by a private person in similar circumstances. Banks manipulated LIBOR in London under circumstances that raise questions about whether government regulators in London may have looked the other way after the American Federal Reserve Bank in New York sent the London regulators a warning.

We see still another disturbing picture when we shift to the question of mind-altering drugs. In some parts of the United States, there is strong sentiment to make marijuana legal. This is already close to the truth in the Netherlands, another country that has had a strong Christian witness in its past. All over the world new intoxicating drugs are being created and old ones used more. All of this disturbs the ability to reason and maintain emotional stability. That in turn damages family life. We cannot total how many family brawls and eventual divorces have been fueled by mind-altering drugs (including alcohol in quantity) but the total must be enormous. As a former part-time public defender I believe that more than half of my defense work was triggered by one or more drugs.

In sum, we all are swimming in a moral cesspool. The very Bible that is almost universally rejected by the younger generations over the world foretells this very thing. *"But evil men will grow worse and worse, deceiving and being deceived."* 2 Timothy 3:13. Widespread violence characterized the world of Noah (Genesis 6:11); the Lord Jesus prophesied that conditions would be similar before He would judge the world. Matthew 24:37. In the next two verses He continued and observed that the world would be taken by surprise by His return. Peter in 2 Peter 2 & 3 informs us that there will be widespread disbelief in Biblical history just before the judgment. Humanity has constructed a virtual universe in the public mind that will ignore God, deny that humanity has been created by God, and deny that an individual is accountable to anyone beyond human institutions for what that individual does or refrains from doing. This unbelief pollutes nearly all contemporary human institutions.

Islam does have a culture radically different from Western secularism. Its fundamental assumption (in its most prominent radical form, although not all Muslims practice this) is that it is one's duty to try to establish a godly kingdom by military force and coercion. This is totally contrary to what the Lord Jesus told Pilate: *"My kingdom is not of this world. If My kingdom were of this world, then would My servants fight."* John 18:36. Our Lord Jesus could have called 12 legions of angels to establish His kingdom then and there had He chosen to do so (Matthew 26:53), but that was premature and not in accord with His plan. Jesus Christ instead chose to establish His Church on earth based on the teachings that He gave to His original apostles and prophets, which we have recorded in the New Testament, which in turn was anticipated by the Old Testament. But the Lord Jesus made it crystal clear that sinful human beings were not to impose His kingdom by political or military force. In history, more evil than good has come from efforts at worldwide conquest. The worst is yet to come in the person and career of the Anti-Christ. One example of this is the Parable of the Tares (in modern language, weeds) found in Matthew 13:24-30 and interpreted in Matthew 13:36-43. He reserves the forcible establishment of His rule for Himself and the angels under His command. This is one of many differences between Islam and Christianity.

I am not saying that individual Christians should remain silent on political subjects. Daniel the prophet was a great Secretary of the Treasury in the early Persian Empire, as Daniel 6 shows. John the Baptist spoke prophetically about a ruler taking his wife from his own brother. He was eventually martyred for his boldness. Matthew 14:1-11. But the Church is not charged with the use of force even though the Church may need to speak out on aspects of politics that implicate Biblical truth. But the Church cannot use force to attempt to establish the rule of Jesus Christ.

What if modern secular assumptions are wrong? Modern secularism assumes that God either does not exist or is functionally absent from human affairs. Biblical Christianity draws from the Holy Bible a set of principles and assumptions totally contrary to any of the world's systems of belief. These principles apply to every human being of every era, technology and culture. Human beings are in fact created by God and will be accountable to Him for what they do and say and also what they refrain from doing or saying. God has established principles by which all human beings will be judged. The price for sin for every believer was paid by Jesus Christ on the Cross.

Modern secular theory assumes a random universe without moral causation. Disasters in this mindset have nothing to do with the moral quality of the persons who suffer. Jesus Christ did in Luke 13:1-5 refute the opposite proposition that natural disasters always fall on the worst people, but He did not say that natural disasters never fall because of moral failure. The Flood came because of the wickedness of the people in Noah's time, as Genesis 6 makes clear. Fire from heaven fell on Sodom and Gomorrah because of their sexual wickedness. Jude 7. The destruction of Pompeii in 79 AD by volcano most probably had a major connection to the wickedness of the city, although this disaster came just after the original composition of most of the New Testament and is not directly mentioned in the Bible. The fall of Babylon in Daniel 5 was a direct result of the insults to God in Belshazzar's party. So there are times when moral evil provokes God to inflict natural disaster. The prophet Joel is another example. When dealing with a direct causal connection between moral wickedness and natural disaster, both extreme answers—"always" and "never"—are wrong. Modern humanists and secularists engage in wishful thinking in clinging to "never."

Biblical Christianity perceives two fundamental classes of people. One believes in Jesus Christ as Lord, has in principle surrendered to

Him and worships Him as God Incarnate. This class makes a serious effort to obey Him and to be like Him, but recognizes that it has no merit of its own for salvation. This class recognizes that each person deserves damnation and is thankful to the Lord Jesus for enduring the punishment that each person of faith fully deserves. The second class does not believe in the Lord Jesus Christ as Lord and Savior. Within this class of persons is a wide variety of beliefs. Some of these beliefs have certain elements of the Bible mixed with man-made doctrines and others have no connection with Christianity whatsoever. In Matthew 25:31-46 these two classes are symbolized as the sheep and the goats.

Both classes of people will have an up-close and personal encounter with Jesus Christ as Judge with His judgment binding without change or appeal throughout eternity. The Bible warns that everyone who does not believe will learn with a shudder that God is indeed angry. The next realization will be that it's personal, that God is angry with <u>me</u>. By then it will be too late. I seek through the Holy Spirit in this book to introduce you to the ramifications of Biblical truth to your personal eternity and also to the eventual end of the various cultures and societies in which we now live. What I am describing is universal to all people of any era, any race or color, any language, any culture and any nation. God is in fact in total control whether we can see it or not. With God there is only one race—the human race. As individual human beings created by God we all will face the Last Judgment.

INTRODUCTION—THE TRUTH
OF LIMITED TIME

Before we enter our introduction to the Last Judgment, we need to discuss briefly a concept foreign to much of modern thought. Younger people regularly show surprise that many actions have consequences that cannot be reversed. Many criminal defendants routinely expect rehearings and revisions. Occasionally justice is on their side, but not often. Outside of courtroom life, many people want to go back and forth about everything from athletic scholarships (occasionally with good reason), contracts for major purchases to marriages. As a T-Mobile commercial put it a few years ago, nobody wants to make binding commitments. But often escaping legal commitments is either expensive or impossible.

By analogy, those religions that believe in reincarnation offer apparently infinite chances for someone to get life right. Admittedly, in these religions a badly lived life may lead to a demotion from a human being to a much lower form of life with a difficult path back, but this notion remains radically different from the irrevocable Last Judgment which is found in Jewish thought and which is especially prominent in Biblical Christianity. Isaiah 66:24 says, *"And they shall go forth, and look upon the carcasses of the men that have transgressed against me: for their worm shall not die, neither shall their fire be quenched; and they shall be an abhorring unto all flesh."* This is a thumbnail sketch of the Lake of Fire that is so prominent in Revelation, combining the basic elements of severe pain and perpetual punishment.

With churches that have their origins in Biblical Christianity we have echoes of the idea of another chance after death. Under the doctrine of indulgences which was prominent in Roman Catholicism during the times of Tetzel, Cajetan and Emperor Charles V of the Holy Roman Empire (Cardinal Wolsey and the young King Henry VIII of England were contemporaries), the typical sinner went to a place called Purgatory where the sinner could either endure enough punishment to induce God to relent or from where a living relative could buy for the dead sinner remission of punishment by buying the indulgence for the sinner's benefit. There was also an ancillary doctrine that the Catholic Church had a surplus of merit which could be applied to the dead sinner's account in exchange for payment or perhaps that such merit could be built up by paid masses or prayers on behalf of the dead. This teaching is foreign to the Scriptures, which make clear that human beings are judged for their own deeds and words; other sinners cannot come to anyone's rescue. Ezekiel 18; Revelation 20:12-13. As Ezekiel 18:4 warns, *"The soul that sins shall die."* This is not just physical death but spiritual death as well. Revelation calls this the "second death." The first death of the body can be undone by resurrection, but nothing can reverse the second death of the soul, which lasts forever and ever. Only the Lord Jesus can ransom a soul. Matthew 20:28.

While there has been no formal repudiation of indulgences by the Roman Catholic authorities, indulgences have not been officially sold for hundreds of years, and it would not be fair to impute this doctrine to contemporary Catholics except where a particular person has defended the medieval doctrine. I point out the history here to show how the idea of other chances after death is not confined to Eastern religions involving reincarnation. Like a theme and variations in music, ideas such as second or multiple chances after death echo through human thought. But any idea must be tested by God's Word, the Holy Scriptures.

On the other end of the spectrum of this world's thought, many people deny human existence after physical death, as if we were like animals. This is a logical conclusion from a different false doctrine, that of random evolution as opposed to God's Creation. If there is no afterlife, there logically can be no concern for Heaven or Hell, although I could imagine that an unbeliever might have some sneaking doubts and hope for some form of reinsurance in case he or she is wrong.

Biblical Christianity rejects both the idea of second chances after physical death and the idea that the soul ceases consciousness when the body dies because the Bible teaches clearly that *"it is appointed to man once to die, and after this the judgment."* Hebrews 9:27. This life is your only opportunity to repent of your sin and to place your faith in Jesus Christ. It's now or never.

Much of the Epistle to the Romans is devoted to proving that human beings can never earn any portion of salvation. Do you want your wages from God—what you have earned? I don't! *"For the wages of sin is death, but the gift of God is eternal life through Jesus Christ our Lord.* Romans 6:23. I have earned death, but instead of my wages God gives me life as His free gift which I have not earned and can never earn. *"Now to him who works the reward is not reckoned of grace but of debt. But to him who does not work but believes on Him who justifies the ungodly, his faith is counted for righteousness . . . Blessed is he whose iniquity is forgiven, whose sin is covered. Blessed is the man to whom the Lord will not impute sin."* Romans 4:4-5, 7-8. For my eternal life, I need mercy, not justice! I need Christ's righteousness in my account, not my own bankrupt <u>ersatz</u> righteousness from fig leaves that I try to palm off as good works from my own sinful heart! I need the heart-lung transplant described in Ezekiel 36:26-27, not some superficial attempt to improve my appearance! (The immediate context is the regathering and salvation of Israel, but remember that we *"are all under sin"* [Romans 3:9] and so our spiritual case is the same whether Jew or Gentile as all of Romans 2-4 teach.)

To take a physical analogy, suppose I were diagnosed accurately with colon cancer. Would any sensible doctor prescribe skin treatment to make me look good to treat this? Not while I'm living! That's what the mortician might do after death. While I am still living and can withstand treatment, something must be done (if possible) inside my body to attack and remove the cancer. The King James version describes ungodly false doctrine as "cancer" (2 Timothy 2:17), but the literal is "gangrene," which spreads and kills far more quickly than cancer. A makeover does nothing to deal with the sin in the human heart that is strangling our souls. It might make it worse if it increases our pride. Instead of the makeover on the outside, we need the divine heart-lung transplant on the inside with the Holy Spirit that breathes in life to replace our deadness. In the physical world we might attempt a makeover ourselves, but not a heart-lung transplant. We need desperately to plead with the Great Physician—Jesus Christ—to do that heart-lung transplant in us. We can no more earn any portion of our salvation than we can perform our own heart-lung transplant.

One of the first things we learn as Christians is that God is in total control of human events. Humanity may do all sorts of things that violate His commandments, but they do nothing beyond His control. Human beings may listen to their own sinful impulses or even to demons, but they remain under the control of God. They will be accountable forever for their attempted and accomplished acts, words and thoughts of disobedience. But whatever their intentions, they will end up serving the purposes of God even if that thought makes the person grit his or her teeth.

For the moment let us go back to late 1776 to deal with a smaller example from American history to get a sense of this truth. Thomas Paine was no friend of Christianity and up to this time had been a failure among human beings. He is generally believed to have been an atheist. Yet he wrote <u>Common Sense</u>, a bolt out of the blue. It was wildly successful in a financial sense, and at a critical moment encouraged American morale just before the Battle of Trenton. Then while the Americans were crossing the Delaware, a Loyalist farmer wrote a note to the commander of the Hessians at Trenton, warning that the Americans were on their way. But Colonel Rall put the note in his pocket instead of reading it right away. The Hessians partied on Christmas night and slept late the next morning as the Americans were marching in from their nighttime river crossing. This is a historical example of how at least two Scriptures have been fulfilled in spiritual terms time and again. *"For the Lord has poured out on you the spirit of deep sleep and has closed your eyes; the prophets and your rulers, the seers He has covered."* Isaiah 29:10, quoted in translation in Romans 11:8. And again, *"His watchmen are blind; they are all ignorant. They are all dumb dogs; they cannot bark, sleeping, lying down, loving to slumber. Yes, they are greedy dogs that can never have enough, and they are shepherds that cannot understand. They all look to their own way, every one for his gain from his quarter. They say, 'You come. I will fetch wine and we will fill ourselves with strong drink, and tomorrow will be as today, and much more abundant.'"* Isaiah 56:10-12. What was true of the Hessian mercenaries in 1776 is also true of many so-called spiritual leaders today. As General Washington and his men swept down by surprise, so most of humanity will be shocked to see—too late to repent—the unmistakeable signs of the Lord Jesus in the process of His descent from heaven to earth to establish His rule of justice and righteousness.

To take another analogy, suppose you are in the process of burglary and you decide that you have had enough of that life as you are rifling the house for valuables. You might be thinking that this is your last job. Then you look out the window and see a police car in front. Then you see another patrol car in the back alley. You may have thought to leave your life of crime, but now it's too late and you have to pay the piper. So it will be for many at the return of the Lord Jesus. *"Behold, now is the accepted time; now is the day of salvation."* 2 Corinthians 6:2.

A third analogy may also help. Most of us have taken standardized tests with strict and inflexible time limits. The proctor will say something like "Time's up" or "Pencils down" at which time one is absolutely required to stop. This concept applies both to our individual lives and to the life of human civilization before the Second Coming of Jesus Christ. Psalm 90 has this basic concept. Even the hairs on our heads are all numbered. Matthew 10:30, Luke 12:7. The Babylonian Empire was terminated by God, using the Media-Persian alliance as His instrument. Daniel 5:26. After his death, Samuel the Prophet told Saul that he would die the next day, which came true. 1 Samuel 28:19.

While circumstances vary, our time will be up soon enough no matter how strong we feel now. *"It is appointed to men once to die and after this the Judgment."* Hebrews 9:27.

Since people do not know the will of God beforehand, their acts have the attributes of free choice even though ultimate results are firmly in God's control. Consider how Peter approached the Crucifixion: *"You men of Israel, hear these words. Jesus of Nazareth, a man approved by God among you by miracles, wonders and signs, which God did by Him in the midst of you, as you yourselves also know. Him, being delivered by the determinate counsel and foreknowledge of God, you have taken and with wicked hands have crucified and killed . . .* (Acts 2:22-23) Peter affirms both that the Crucifixion was predetermined by God and that the perpetrators of the Crucifixion are guilty of shedding innocent blood. Judas is a similar case. His betrayal was prophesied (Psalm 41:9) and yet Judas was fully responsible for his conduct. Luke 17:1. Because we lack specific knowledge of our own future, the sovereignty of God and human responsibility can and do coexist. This will become crystal clear at the Last Judgment.

A BRIEF INTRODUCTORY
NOTE ON HUMAN RIGHTS

In modern debate issues are cast as human rights. But from where do human rights come? If they come from human consensus, they have no stable foundation. The Communist world has recognized almost no human rights for the common citizen. The Nazis obliterated human rights for Jews by defining them as sub-human. Their view of Slavic peoples was not much better. Islamic political theory leans strongly toward dictatorship, sacrificing freedom for the sake of dictated order. So did the theory of "divine right of kings" prevalent in Europe in the Middle Ages. Surely order is an improvement over anarchy; this is why God instituted human government after the Flood in the first place. But on this theory who or what restrains the rulers? Rulers are likewise sinners who require restraint just as much as the common people. In fact, with the temptations of power rulers probably require more restraint. It was this point that the advocates of the divine right of kings or other dictatorship missed, whether they came from England such as Thomas Hobbes or from other parts of the globe. No sinful human being can be trusted with unrestrained power. The Nazis and the various Communist regimes are simply the most vivid modern examples of this truth found in the Scriptures (for example, 1 Samuel 8) and proved true by history.

So who defines human rights? Since humanity cannot do so, that leaves God as the source of human rights. First is the right to life, given at Creation and memorialized in the Sixth Commandment against murder. Economic life and incentives are made possible by private property, given by God and memorialized by the Seventh Commandment against stealing and the Tenth Commandment against coveting. The right of people of suitable age to marry is protected by the Eighth Commandment against adultery. The Scriptures are careful to define this as the right to marry and live with one person of the opposite sex. This is not a right to marry just anyone. If someone is already married, he or she is off limits. The Bible recognizes no human right to same-sex marriages and in fact records the destruction of a society that tolerated same-sex relationships with judgment by fire from heaven. Man was not the source of destruction—that source was God Almighty. (See Genesis 18 & 19.)

Further, the right to marry does not include the right to cohabit without marriage. God has linked sexual intercourse with relationships that last for the joint lives of the marriage partners. For a particularly strong example, see Deuteronomy 22:28-29.

The Bible does recognize the virtues of debate, both in Acts 15 and in Proverbs 25:9 and in Proverbs 18:17. But again there are limits. As human beings created by God and in the image of God and as depending on Him for our survival, we have no human right to curse and blaspheme His name. This definite limit is found in the Third Commandment.

When we speak of human rights, we cannot speak of any rights which restrain God Himself. As sinless, He needs no restraint. Consider what the Bible says about our right to live in the Lord Jesus' Parable of the Rich Farmer. God said to the farmer, *"You fool! Tonight your soul will be required of you, and then whose shall thes thing be, which you have provided?"* Luke 12:20. So God has the authority, the power and the right to take our life and anything that we own without question or argument. King Nebuchadnezzar lost his sanity and his royal power for 7 years (Daniel 4) and then they were restored at God's pleasure. The Apostle Paul frequently introduced himself as God's slave. Our faith must be in God and in His mercy, not in any rights we claim to limit Him.

Since God is the source of human rights and defines them Himself, we will have no claim to immunity from His Law when He judges us. Remember that we face judgment both for what we did and said and also for what we did not do and for our silence when it was our responsibility to speak. *"If you forbear to deliver [those] drawn to death and ready to be killed; If you say, 'Behold, we did not know it,' does not He that ponders the heart consider? And He that keeps your soul, does He know it? And shall He render to man according to his works?"* The obvious answer to these rhetorical questions is "yes." God defines the principles of judgment without regard to what we may think. We all fall short of the glory of God and face His judgment, either with the protection of the Blood of Jesus Christ sacrificed for sin or with no protection at all.

ASPECTS OF THE CHARACTER OF GOD

In today's world most people think of God as an indulgent rich grandfather if they think of Him at all. There is just enough truth in this view to make it dangerous. God's riches are indeed beyond description. *"Every beast of the forest is Mine, and the cattle on a thousand hills."* Psalm 50:10. *"The earth is the Lord's and the fullness of it."* Psalm 24:1. Yes, He has created us to manage and use it for His glory and for our benefit. We have our oxygen and our water given to us in the right proportions. The force of gravity is just right for us to survive and thrive. We have the silicon we need to make computers, the iron we need to make steel and hydrocarbons for fuel, plastics and a host of other products. Nitrogen in the atmosphere is benign and a critical component of ammonia and fertilizer. At our most intelligent, we make use of elements and properties that God has stocked ahead of time for our use. With the increase of knowledge predicted by the prophet Daniel, we still have not begun to fathom all that God has done for us in the ocean. We still should cry out with Solomon, *"The heaven of heavens cannot contain You—how much less this house that I have built."* 1 Kings 8:27. Or as Paul said, *"O the depths of the riches of both the wisdom and knowledge of God! How unsearchable are His judgments, and His ways past finding out. For who has known the mind of the Lord, or who has been His counsellor? Or who first has given to Him, that it should be recompensed to him again? For of Him, and to Him, and to Him are all things, to Whom be glory forever! Amen.* Romans 11:33-36.

God also gave us friendships and marriage between man and woman to give companionship in addition to our fellowship with Himself.

But what have we done with His gifts? From the Garden of Eden we have disobeyed, starting with Adam. Both moral and physical pollution stem from that original sin and the rebellion that most people have waged against God ever since. The very process of living generates waste from birth forward. Try as we might, we can no more generate a completely non-polluting economy than we can obey in full the Ten Commandments. We still have some joyous though imperfect marriages, but our society is in the process of distorting God's original gift of marriage between one man and one woman beyond recognition. What is more, as a whole our society flaunts our multiple sins in God's face as if we were *torreadors* taunting a bull to charge. We curse His name and the name of His Son Jesus Christ almost naturally as we breathe. In some jurisdictions such as Washington, D.C. and Delaware (using 2008 figures) about 30% of all children conceived are murdered by abortion. When one adds the rising number of suicides, we are rejecting His gift of life itself in alarming numbers. This is not merely an American problem. While there is some recent change afoot, China has actually compelled millions of mothers to undergo abortions against their will in the name of population control. Sex-selective abortions are spreading through Asia, killing females because of their expensive dowries when they grow up and marry.

And how does our society expect God to react? Perhaps not at all or perhaps with an indulgent wink. Boys will be boys and girls will do their thing. But what about this expectation? If it is wrong, most human beings are in deadly peril, not only for this life but also for eternity. So let us examine the Bible to see if God is as indulgent as we are prone to imagine, starting with instances of particular individuals or small groups. Then we should come back and consider at least 5 large judgments: Noah's Flood, the judgment of the Canaanites in the time of Joshua, the fall of the Northern Kingdom of Israel to Assyria, the fall of the Southern Kingdom of Judah to Nebuchadnezzar and the fall of the Jerusalem where the Lord Jesus preached to Rome.

Er & Onan (**Genesis 38:1-10**) This involved two of Jacob's grandchildren, sons of his son Judah. The Scriptures simply state that Er was wicked without further explanation. For our purpose of exploring aspects of the character of God that are commonly omitted even from Christian teaching, the important point is God's reaction to Er's wickedness rather than the specifics of that wickedness. God struck Er dead. We know that a human being can provoke God sufficiently to trigger his or her own immediate death. God abhors sin and is angry when sin is flaunted at Him. (Psalm 7:10-17; Jeremiah 2:32-36. Note also the contrary result of Proverbs 28:13, where God extends mercy when sin is admitted and forsaken.)

We know more about the specifics of Onan's offense. Under ancient law later codified in the Law of Moses, Onan was under obligation to marry Er's widow and with her father a child for Er because Er had died childless. Onan deliberately disregarded this duty. For this reason God killed Onan also. This confirms what we can observe about part of God's character that we can see in Er's case.

Absalom (**2 Samuel 13-19**) Absalom was one of the most prominent sons of David. Of his older sons, Absalom seems to have displayed the most drive and ability to rule. But the most critical element, the love of God that was present in David, was missing from Absalom. So as we survey these chapters, we can see that God pursued Absalom to his death because of Absalom's sin. In fact, Absalom's potentially good qualities such as his initiative and vigor would have made the damage worse had God permitted these qualities to operate to their full effectiveness.

We first see Absalom after David's great sin involving Uriah and Bath-sheba. One of David's sons, Amnon, had a crush on Tamar, Absalom's sister. So Amnon pretended to be sick and asked that Tamar bring him food. She did so. Amnon raped Tamar and then discarded her as worthless. Absalom waited for his opportunity and then avenged Tamar's rape by killing Amnon. Thus far, Absalom was able to claim some justification for his actions, as rape under the Law of Moses called for the death penalty. King David was remiss in not so punishing Amnon even though Amnon was one of David's sons. David was probably reluctant to enforce the Law of Moses against Amnon because David had earlier committed his own capital crimes in murdering Uriah after committing adultery with Uriah's wife.

Absalom fled after striking down Amnon, but Joab (David's army commander) arranged to bring Absalom back. By this time Absalom's ambition had gone far beyond avenging Tamar to the throne of Israel itself. He started by complaining (probably with some justification) that David was not paying enough attention to the administration of justice within Israel (2 Samuel 15:1-6). It was but a short leopard's spring from this to outright revolt. Absalom even took possession of some of his father's wives as a sign to Israel that there was no turning back.

But God did not approve of Absalom's revolt against his father, even though God did not approve of David's failings either and chastised David severely (Psalm 38, 118:18) for them. Joab now realized that in bringing back Absalom that he had created a monster. So God arranged for one of David's supporters to act as a spy and to persuade Absalom to take time to marshal an overwhelming force (2 Samuel 15-16), giving David time to escape and secure supplies. When the battle was joined, God overruled David's orders to spare Absalom by causing Absalom's hair—his pride and joy—to get tangled in a tree. A soldier found Absalom and brought Joab, who was wise enough to kill the rebel immediately so that the fighting could be stopped. In this case God destroyed Absalom in stages rather than with a single blow, but it remains true that God made sure of Absalom's downfall and death. We have not been created by a passive God but by the Almighty God Who intervenes in and controls human affairs. With the death of Absalom and later by the defeat of Adonijah (1 Kings 1-3, especially Adonijah's own confession in 1 Kings 2:13-15) God made sure that Solomon succeeded David as King of Israel.

In Absalom's life we have seen that God's judgment can be just as thorough if done slowly as if done speedily. A contrast to the slow, methodical judgment upon Absalom was the swift and violent judgment visited upon a crowd of teenagers who taunted Elisha the prophet about his baldness. (2 Kings 2:23-24) Two female bears behaved as if their cubs were threatened and killed 42 of the crowd. God reserves the right to visit the ultimate penalty of immediate death for sin.

Gehazi: Under the Old Covenant, normally the children of Israel were the objects of God's favor more than other peoples, because they had more revelation about the one true God. Yet this was not invariably true. Naaman the Syrian was the only person healed of leprosy through Elisha the prophet. (See Luke 4:27 for confirmation.) When Gehazi tried to make a financial profit from the healing and then attempted to cover his tracks, he was sentenced by Elisha to contract the leprosy of Naaman. This was in effect a sentence to strict quarantine (almost solitary confinement) and isolation followed by a slow, painful death. While the start of the judgment was immediate, its effects in this case made themselves fully felt over time. God imposes different judgments as He sees is right, but Gehazi is another case where the start of the judgment was immediate.

Ahab & Jezebel: Ahab was judged for his complicity in the scheme of his wife Jezebel in framing Naboth on false charges of blasphemy in order to steal his vineyard. In contrast to Gehazi, neither Ahab nor Jezebel were judged immediately. But we should never assume that anyone will get away with sin because divine justice seems to be delayed in a given case. A few years later Ahab was mortally wounded by a stray arrow in battle. A few more years later Jezebel was trampled alive by Jehu's warhorses. Though the judgments were delayed, they were sure and thorough. If in your personal case God's judgment seems to be delayed, then plead with Him for mercy through the blood of His Son Jesus Christ in repentance and faith. Perhaps God is opening the door to you for forgiveness based on the only way sin can be washed away—the blood of the perfect Passover sacrifice, Jesus the Messiah (in Greek, the Christ).

Baruch: In contrast to the previous examples where God intervened to punish and judge sin, Baruch is a case where God intervened to protect a faithful servant. He was Jeremiah's secretary and assistant, as shown in Jeremiah 32:12 and 36:4. In Jeremiah 45 as Judah was about to go into complete captivity, God gave Baruch instructions that he was not to seek great things for himself. God knew that such was impossible. But God did promise that Baruch's life would be spared. In a time of slaughter, this was of great comfort and value. While our present subject is the judgment of God, we should remember that God is equally capable of mercy and protection as He is of judgment. Even in the Book of Lamentations written by Jeremiah there are passages of hope. So at this time there remains hope for any person who will seek God on His terms.

Haman: Haman is another example of God's judgment but also of hope for those who have faith in Him. When the Persian Empire was strong, Haman proposed to contribute a massive part of the state budget in exchange for the privilege of killing and then plundering every Jew within the Persian Empire. This sounds very much like an ancient Holocaust. The king initially gave permission, but Mordecai and Esther protested and Esther herself presented her case to the King. Haman pleaded with Esther for his life, which the King took to be an attempt upon the virtue of Queen Esther. Haman was hanged summarily as attempting to rape Esther, which was the wrong crime. In truth he was guilty of attempted mass murder, including of Queen Esther, and merited hanging many times over as did the top Nazis at Nuremburg. Haman's ten sons were hanged in order to remove any source of revenge. The Jews were given permission to defend themselves against their enemies, which they exercised with relish. So Mordecai and Queen Esther and the entire nation in exile and in Israel under Persian control were delivered and the guilty plotters perished. This is only a thumbnail of the Book of Esther, but it amply illustrates the active intervention of God in human history to save and to destroy.

Amaziah: One of the false priests of the Northern Kingdom was named Amaziah. He bore the same name as a king of Judah and as a different king of the Northern Kingdom, but he was not the same man as either of those kings. Nevertheless, he bore a spiritual likeness to those two evil kings. Amos was warning the people in the capital of the Northern Kingdom of the coming judgment from God. Amaziah represented the official royal religion of the Northern Kingdom, which had been formed to divert Jews in the Northern Kingdom from going to Jerusalem as Moses had commanded. When Amos called for repentance, this particular Amaziah told Amos in so many words to shut up, leave the capital and indeed leave the country and go to Judah, which at this period was somewhat faithful to God. Amos retorted in Amos 7:17 that Amaziah the false priest would see his children killed and his wife prostitute herself in the streets as a judgment for his treatment of Amos. He himself would lose his land and die in exile.

Zedekiah: Zedekiah was the last king of Judah. The end of his story is found in 2 Kings 25. Originally he had sworn allegiance to the King of Babylon as a vassal. Jeremiah had likewise advised submission to Babylon as a prophet of God, but Zedekiah chose the path of rebellion instead. He was not given an immediate death sentence, but the Babylonians chose to make an example of Zedekiah. The last thing that Zedekiah saw was the execution of his 10 sons by the Babylonians. Then Zedekiah himself was blinded and led away in fetters. We hear nothing further about Zedekiah. One of his predecessors, former King Jehoiachin, who also was taken captive by Babylon was eventually treated kindly in his later years of exile. But by its very nature the judgment upon Zedekiah could not be reversed; his 10 children could not be brought back to life nor his sight restored. These judgments were administered by human beings but with the permission of God Almighty. Zedekiah is an example where his sin triggered judgments that were final and not subject to revision.

Another set of instances of God's direct intervention into tiny portions of His Creation are found in the life of Jonah. From the great fish to the gourd, God was in complete and precise control.

Ananias & Sapphira: These warnings of personal judgment are not confined to the Old Testament. In Acts 5, Ananias and Sapphira conspired to lie to Peter and to the Holy Spirit about the price they had received for selling a parcel of land. The gist of their sin was trying to pass off a partial contribution of the proceeds as if what they contributed was the full price. Obviously the Holy Spirit was not fooled, and neither was Peter as an apostle led by the Holy Spirit. To modern readers, the sentence of immediate death upon both Ananias and Sapphira seems shockingly harsh. However, it is a reminder of the holiness of God and of the futility and seriousness of trying to deceive God. If upon reflection we still think that God was unfair, then we can be sure that we need again to reflect on the first portion of Romans 6:23: *"the wages of sin is death."*

Herod: There is a second instance dealing with a local king under Roman authority named Herod, who was a nephew of the Herod that built the Temple that existed in Jesus' time and who commanded the soldiers to kill the newborn males near Bethlehem in order to make sure of killing the Lord Jesus. The more recent Herod's story is told in Acts 12. He killed James and was going to kill Peter also but was prevented from killing Peter by angelic intervention. This Herod had had a dispute with a neighboring province, which was to be settled by Herod giving an oration and then the people would acclaim Herod as a god. But the real God in heaven did not join the applause. Instead, when the earthling Herod received the acclamation as if he were a god, the God of Heaven struck Herod with worms and killed him as an example to other human beings not to accept worship. Nero did not heed the warning and was forced to commit suicide to avoid being killed by his own guards. Later Roman Emperors demanded worship also. Some, like Nero, died quickly. Others, perhaps more circumspect, lived more normal life spans. But God's testimony against the worship of any emperor was established in His immediate and obvious judgment against this Herod and then against Nero.

Bar-jesus/Elymas: Continuing in Acts to chapter 13, we find another case of judgment for interfering with the plan of God, although the judgment was less severe. Paul and Barnabas were explaining the Gospel to Sergius Paulus, a Roman official. A magician (probably a practitioner of the occult) tried to interfere. Through Paul God judged the magician with temporary blindness. Once again we do not know whether the magician ever repented of his sins, and in this case the blindness was not said to be permanent. Nevertheless, this is another instance of God's direct intervention with human beings.

There are many illustrations of God's intervention in the lives of human beings, for blessing as well as for judgment. Ananias and Sapphira are examples of God's judgment within His church. Philip was sent to show the Savior Jesus Christ to the Ethopian on the desert road. The Apostle Paul is an example of God carrying out His choice of an apostle from among Jesus' most vociferous enemies. Cornelius the centurion was chosen to be the first Gentile to hear the Gospel from Peter. Peter was rescued from jail the night before his scheduled execution. Paul was directed away from Asia Minor into Macedonia by a dream. This led Paul to Philippi. One could go on, but the basic idea is to scan the Book of Acts for instances of God's intervention directly into the lives of individuals.

While we are not given names of individuals we are informed in 1 Corinthians 11:30 that many people in the church in Corinth were dead because of abuse of the Lord's Table. In Revelation 2:20, the Lord Jesus threatened a particular woman in Thyatira with grievous sickness and her children with death unless she repented of her sins. I am unsure whether this woman was originally named Jezebel or whether the Lord Jesus fastened upon her the spiritual name of Jezebel. For present purposes, we do not need to know that detail. In either case we know that the Lord Jesus personally threatened a particularly sinful woman with judgments direct from heaven as a last warning for her to repent of her sins and change direction drastically.

Briefly we shift our survey from individual judgments to mass judgments of large numbers of people. Noah's Flood is the first such case. The only survivors from the entire human race were Noah, his wife, their three sons (Shem, Ham and Japheth) and their wives. This is affirmed in 1 Peter 3:20. Interestingly, the genetic unity of the human race as it now lives on earth confirms the basic idea that currently living humanity stems from very few people instead of independent instances of alleged evolution. The Biblical account of the Flood leaving few survivors is basically consistent with what our investigation of the human genome is showing. The Lord Jesus also confirms the account of Noah's Flood. Luke 17:26-27; Matthew 24:37-38.

Next in time is the fall of the Northern Kingdom of Israel to Assyria. The reasons why God allowed this are found in detail in 2 Kings 17:7-18, dealing both with evil worship and evil conduct. The consequence was that *"The Lord was very angry with Israel and removed them out of His sight."* 2 Kings 17:18. We will have to focus more closely on the anger of God later, but for the moment we must note that the conduct of the Northern Kingdom provoked God to severe anger that He actually expressed by removing His protection and bringing their cruel enemies on them. In contrast, God by miracle saved Judah from Assyrian conquest during the time of Hezekiah, although damage from Assyrian invasion was severe. For that contrasting account review Isaiah 35-39, 2 Kings 18:13-19:37 and 2 Chronicles 32:1-23.

But Judah did not remain faithful to God either. During the reign of Hezekiah's son Manasseh Judah became subservient to Assyria and extremely wicked also. Ezekiel 16 contains an extended explanation of God's judgment upon Judah. Ezekiel 16:51-52 appears to say that Judah became even worse than the Northern Kingdom. 2 Kings 21 and 23:25-27 contain a concise explanation for the judgment of Judah notwithstanding the righteous measures of King Josiah, a truly godly king like Hezekiah and David before him. 2 Chronicles 36:11-21 contains another summary of the reasons for judging Judah, focusing on the sins of King Zedekiah and his contemporaries but also serving as a summary of Judah's overall decline after Solomon's death. One could also review Jeremiah 2 and 5 for still another angle of vision. Since I am trying to deal with God's judgment as applicable to our own time, I will by-pass a more complete study of the fall of Judah and the reasons for it, although that would be a spiritually and historically useful study all by itself.

For another miniature of the effects of the Last Judgment, let us consider Jericho. Joshua is cast as the conquering leader bringing the wrath of God against the wicked city. In the case of Jericho, even the animals and the clothing were to be burned because of the great wickedness of the city. If the region around Sodom and Gomorrah was the original area that God judged with a policy of scorched earth, then Jericho is a successor undergoing like treatment. If we look forward to Revelation 20:9, the last army to surround and threaten the saints is exterminated with fire from heaven. While Joshua's fire was not from heaven, it was deadly. *"Our God is a consuming fire."* Hebrews 12:29, quoting Deuteronomy 4:24.

Jericho trusted in its walls and the obstacles outside the walls. These were advanced for that day, with attackers forced to climb a slippery slope to reach the wall. But God demolished these defenses at His appointed time. Inside the walls, the morale of Jericho was low because the inhabitants had heard about the miracles that allowed the people of Israel to escape Egypt. With one exception that resulted in a trial and death for disobedience (see the account of the trial of Achan in Joshua 7), the Israelites obeyed the orders of God through Joshua to destroy everything without taking booty. The time for judgment had come. The disobedient soldier and his family members were executed for their disobedience and complicity in hiding the stolen and buried treasure.

So Joshua is a forerunner of Jesus in His Second Coming as a conqueror and bringer of judgment. He was not perfect, but in the main he carried out God's orders to destroy the wicked inhabitants of Canaan to make way for God's people Israel. Joshua insisted that all of Israel serve the true God (Joshua 24:15), and during his own time they remained faithful. Joshua 24:31. In fact the name Jesus is derived from the name Joshua. Both were deliverers who led their people into the Promised Land.

There is one other similarity among the Old Testament judgments. When the pre-Flood population was destroyed, there was a tiny remnant that received grace and escaped. This was the family of Noah. A total of eight people were spared destruction in the Flood. When Sodom and Gomorrah were destroyed by fire from heaven (God kept His promise not to flood the earth again, so fire was the destroying agent), there was also a tiny remnant who escaped. This remnant was composed of righteous Lot and his two daughters. Lot's wife escaped the city limits but was turned into a pillar of salt when she looked back longingly at Sodom.

If we come forward in time to Jericho, once more we find a remnant. Jericho was so wicked that God chose to save a woman with a sordid past. At a very minimum Rahab was a prostitute; I understand the Bible text to imply that she was a madam who used her lodging house as a brothel. Was this the best Jericho could offer? I don't know that. God saves according to His choice rather than on any concept of comparative merit. But if one person and her family were to be saved from the destruction of Jericho, Rahab was an unlikely choice (just as Saul of Tarsus was an unlikely choice to become an Apostle).

Despite her wicked past Rahab grasped the essentials of faith. This cannot be accounted for by mere intelligence. One can be sure that the commanders of Jericho's defense were intelligent men. Consider what Rahab said to the spies starting in Joshua 2:9: *"I know that the Lord has given you the land, and that your terror has fallen on us, and that all of the inhabitants of the land faint because of you. For we have heard how the Lord dried up the water of the Red Sea for you when you came out of Egypt, and what you did to the two kings of the Amorites who were on the other side of Jordan, Sihon and Og whom you utterly destroyed. And as soon as we heard, our hearts melted. Neither did any more courage remain in any man because of you. For the Lord your God—He is God in heaven above and in earth beneath."* Joshua 2:9-11. So the foundation of Rahab's petition for deliverance from destruction which begins in verse 12 was faith. Rahab probably had no Bible at all. Moses was just recently dead and his writings would not have yet circulated. I believe that the events of Job had long occurred, but there is no indication that Rahab was aware of them. So Rahab had only the testimony of witnesses who had passed in and out of Jericho before the spies. Let us consider what she believed, comparing it in particular to what Paul says that humanity knows by conscience in Romans 1. There Paul lists God's *eternal power and Godhead, so that [people generally] are without excuse."* Romans 1:20. Rahab recognized how God had dried up the

Red Sea. She apparently did not know how God had dried the Jordan just before the army of Israel marched on Jericho. But with the example of the Red Sea Rahab recognized His power. Then she also confessed that He is God everywhere, in heaven and throughout the earth. This reflects the cries of the witnesses to the fire from heaven that consumed Elijah's sacrifice. *"The Lord, He is the [only] God! The Lord, He is the [only] God!"* 1 Kings 18:39.

So Rahab was delivered from the just punishment of her sins by the grace of God through faith. Perhaps God chose her to show us that salvation by grace through faith is available not only to the respectable but also even to the horrible. The violent robber who was saved while dying on his cross shows the same principle. Rahab showed her faith by hiding the spies and deceiving the authorities looking for them, somewhat as Corrie ten Boom deceived the Nazis and hid Jews marked for extermination. In Corrie's case, her acts were an extension of an established pattern of an upright life. In Rahab's case, her actions showed an abrupt change of heart caused by God through sensible and well-founded fear which ripened into faith. The Lord Jesus placed His stamp of approval on the transformed Rahab by choosing her as one of His human ancestors in His family tree. Once again when the Lord Jesus returns to earth as judgments are crashing down, a remnant including the nation of Israel will be spared by God's mercy.

As shown by Matthew 24, Mark 13 and Luke 21, the closest analogy of all to the coming judgment of the earth and its former and present inhabitants is the conquest of Jerusalem by Roman armies in 70 AD. In these recordings of Jesus' teachings about the Temple, Israel and the Last Judgment, the micro-judgment of Jerusalem (still one of the most horrifying sieges in history—perhaps the Leningrad [now reverted to its traditonal name of St. Petersburg] siege of 1941-44 by the Nazis is the closest parallel in modern history) is a miniature of the worldwide judgment to come. Notice the combination of questions in Matthew 24:1-3. Josephus' description of the siege is historical testimony of the fulfillment of the curses of which Moses warned in Deuteronomy 4:15-40, Deuteronomy 28 and Deuteronomy 32:1-43. God described

Himself in Deuteronomy 32:39: *"See now that I, I am He, and there is no god with Me. I kill and I make alive. I wound and I heal. Neither is there any that can deliver out of My hand."* If you were to continue with Deuteronomy 32:40-43, you can see a Messianic prophecy of Jesus Christ delivering both Israel as a nation and His worshippers among the Gentiles as would later be unveiled in Zechariah (portions of 9-14) and in Revelation starting with chapter 4.

I have not even come close to a complete list of God's direct interventions into human affairs as described in the Bible, let alone those mentioned in history outside the Bible. This listing is sufficient for modern humanity to re-examine and discard its assumption that it will never have to answer for its conduct, words and thoughts to any higher authority. In 2 Peter 2 and 3, Peter predicts that people will deliberately forget three events showing God's intervention: (1) The judgment of Sodom and Gomorrah and the surrounding regions for sexual immorality, including but not necessarily limited to same-sex practices; (2) The deliverance of righteous Lot from Sodom along with his two daughters; and (3) Noah's Flood in which the entire human race then living was exterminated with the exception of eight people. This wilful ignorance in turn will result in spiritual blindness to God's judgment of this earth and the entire universe and all of its people yet to come. I pray that God would use this book as one instrument in His hand to turn the eyes of people from blindness to spiritual sight before the judgment falls.

A SKETCH OF ONE EMOTION OF GOD: HIS ANGER

When we picture God the Father or Jesus the Son of God, rarely do we think of anger as part of the emotional makeup of either Father or Son. But the Scriptures do warn of God's anger (in older translations, His wrath). *"God judges the righteous, and God is angry [with the wicked] every day."* Psalm 7:11. In Nahum 1:2, we read, *"God is jealous and the Lord revenges; the Lord revenges and is furious. The Lord will take vengeance on His adversaries and reserves [wrath] for His enemies.* In Nahum 1:6 the prophet asks, *"Who can stand before His indignation and who can abide in the fierceness of His anger?"* It is also true that in the next verse Nahum does give promises for the true believers in God, but in the verse after the prophet repeats his solemn warning a third time: *"The Lord is good, a stronghold in the day of trouble, and He knows those who trust in Him. But with an overrunning flood He will make an utter end of the place thereof, and He shall pursue His enemies."*

Can this picture of an angry God coexist with the truth that God is love (1 John 4:8)? Yes! Because of the sin of humanity, love for some must necessarily mean anger directed toward others. Certainly the rescue of the surviving Jews in 1945 had to mean the destruction of the Nazis. A scholar who has studied the surviving sermons of Jonathan Edwards believes that fewer than a dozen out of about 1000 sermons were about hellfire, damnation or judgment. Jonathan Edwards was a pastor but also a top intellectual of his time, quite possibly on a par with Benjamin Franklin, whose life overlapped his. Edwards was President of Princeton University when he died of side effects of a smallpox vaccination which he took in support of medical science. Yet Jonathan Edwards is best remembered for his sermon "Sinners in the Hands of an Angry God" because God used that sermon to spark a religious revival in the American colonies. It was extremely rare for Edwards to preach in that manner, and this sermon was no doubt followed up by many others on the salvation, love and mercy of God. George Whitefield likewise contributed to revivals in the American colonies. So it is not historically accurate to celebrate just one sermon or even one man as having supported a revival alone. Nevertheless, the Holy Spirit led a mild-mannered intellectual to preach out of his normal character in order to wake people up who were spiritually asleep in the face of deadly danger, in the manner that a carbon monoxide alarm will wake up homeowners in time to escape silent, odorless but deadly fumes.

You should ask: it is well enough to argue from history, but should we not demand proof from the Holy Scripture as better proof than history? Correct! So let us consider the Lord Jesus, who was a walking demonstration of love while on earth. Jesus Christ fed 5000 men and their families on one occasion and 4000 men and their families on another. He raised three people from the dead. He healed 10 lepers at once. He healed the blind and cast out demons from an insane man that lived in a cemetery. We cannot count how many people He healed from either physical or mental illness or both. Nobody has matched the Lord Jesus for love and compassion, most especially when He deliberately put His own body on the line to pay for the sins of many who by nature were His enemies. (1 Peter 2:24, Romans 5:8-10; Matthew 20:28)

And yet the Lord Jesus described Himself as angry in Luke 19:12-27. In this parable a hated ruler receives another country to rule, so he is leaving temporarily his first realm to set the second in order. Three men are given money to invest in the interval. Two are faithful and are rewarded. The third was fearful and buried the money. Meanwhile the ruler's original subjects hated him as much as ever when he returned to his original domain. So the owner stripped the fearful one of his responsibilities and cast him into outer darkness (see Matthew 25:30 for the condemnation of the fearful servant in a parallel parable) and also ordered the execution of all of his rebellious subjects. These executions in the parable are a warning of the executions that the returning Lord Jesus will order upon His return to this earth. It is obvious that the Lord Jesus is angry.

A second example is Matthew 22:1-14 (note also a similar parable in Luke 14:15-24), dealing with a ruler (representing God Almighty) Who invited His subjects to celebrate the marriage of His Son. In both parables we see the refusals by the original invitees. In Matthew the detail is added that some of those invited not only snubbed the ruler but actually killed the messengers, as many of the prophets had been killed in the previous history of Israel. So the original invitees who refused the invitation were thereafter excluded. When in Revelation 19:7-9 we see the marriage supper of the Lamb of God, we should understand that the parable is dealing with eternal judgment and not merely a missed opportunity for festivities. God invites us now to the marriage supper of His Son; if we do not repent and believe in His name now we will be forever excluded later. For now we have the offer of divine grace, but if we refuse His invitation now we shall face His perpetual anger later.

This does not come close to exhausting the subject, but it does show us that in painting our mental portrait of the Trinity we must include both love and anger to have any hope of workable accuracy.

A BRIEF SKETCH OF
DIVINE JUSTICE

Wishful thinking leads mean who profess to be Christians to deny the reality of everlasting punishment. Perhaps too many of their family and friends are headed away from Jesus Christ for them to embrace what the Bible teaches on the subject. If Senator Portman would come to approve gay marriage because his son is gay, then surely many would deny eternal punishment to avoid coming to grips with the rebellion against God (whether expressed in any form of sexual relations outside of marriage or expressed in other conduct such as murder, drugs, stealing, slander, false worship, etc.) among their circles of family and friends. But God's standards of character and conduct do not change with human opinion, whether within our family or in the general population. *"Let God be true, although every man may be a liar."* Romans 3:4.

When I was a senior in college at home for spring break, I remember an older guest preacher introduce his sermon subject of "The Judgment of God" by saying that he made no apology for his subject. At the time I was puzzled that he would even think it necessary to explain his choice of the topic and concluded that he had been "stung" somewhere. Apparently he had already experienced resistance to the frank preaching of God's Word. At any rate he was far wiser than I in appreciating the distaste of many for the truth of what the Lord Jesus taught on the subject, most especially in Matthew. Now about 40 years later I am aware that rebellion against the Bible is far more widespread now than it was then. God remembers the preacher's name; I do not. But I salute his steadfastness in teaching the whole truth and the farsightedness of his warning, even though I was only dimly aware of how necessary it was at the time I heard it.

The question occurs to me and (I'm sure) to many others: why cannot God simply annihilate the unbelievers instead of punishing them forever? For one answer, let's go back to Creation. Men and women were made in the image of God (Genesis 1:26-27). One of the essential attributes of God is that He will never die as God. Our Lord Jesus died as a Man, but He never ceased to exist even when His human body lay in the grave borrowed from Joseph of Arimathaea. Our Lord Jesus told the repentant thief, *"Today you shall be with Me in Paradise."* Luke 23:43. Since we humans are made in the image of God, we also have the attribute of perpetual existence and consciousness. Even our need for sleep is temporary; either in heaven or in the Lake of Fire we will no longer sleep. So perpetual awareness is part of the image that we have received from God. To annihilate anyone made in the image of God would contradict what God did at Creation. Like human beings, angels also never cease to exist.

A second reason is that annihilation does not meet the requirements of divine justice. Let's take the sin of murder as a representative case because the reasoning is easiest to see. Murder of one human being by another, such as Cain killing Abel, involves shedding the blood of a person who has been created by God (Psalm 139:13-14) in His image. This applies to modern abortion as it did to Cain. Murder of a human is unlike even the wanton killing of an animal. We cannot value the life of a human being in money, for a human being is far more than his or her labor or wealth. *"What shall it profit a man if he gain the whole world and lose his own soul? Or what shall a man exchange for his soul?"* Mark 8:36-37. Annihilation after death—even death by capital punishment—does not begin to be a proportionate punishment for the murder of a human being bearing the image of God against His express command. We have the two-fold violation:

1   The crime against the life of a person bearing the image of God; and

2   The crime against the command of the eternal God.

Both of these offenses call for eternal punishment if there is no atonement because the offense is against an eternal God. Even in human terms, we understand that offenses either by a ruler (for example, Hitler, Goering and Saddam Hussein) or against a ruler (for example, the assassinations of Lincoln, Garfield, McKinley and Kennedy in the United States) are more serious than ordinary crimes as judged in human courts. So every offense, not murder only, is against a command of the eternal God And God is a God of justice and vengeance as well as a God of mercy.

If neither of these reasons give you any comfort, I'm sure that God has many more that have entirely escaped my understanding. I must simply ask you to accept what God says as true and right by faith even if it runs against your grain. God in heaven is smarter than all human beings (other than Jesus Christ) put together. John the Baptist, the greatest of all the prophets, acknowledged that he was not worthy to even untie Jesus' shoe (John 1:27). There are many things that we cannot now fully understand while on this earth. We must accept the total authority of the Father, Son and Holy Spirit by faith.

We cannot try to evade what God has said about eternal judgment and punishment by attributing it to one or two verses that can somehow be misunderstood. It is a theme that runs through the Bible and especially through the teaching of Jesus Christ. If you disbelieve the doctrines of Hell and eternal punishment, you must then accuse Jesus Christ of being a spiritual liar and a false teacher, as the following sampling of Bible verses will illustrate. This is not a complete list. For example, the Apostle Paul throughout the first portion of Romans assumes a judgment after death without giving detail as to the punishment. But this should be sufficient to show that the doctrine of everlasting punishment of the unrighteous is a major teaching of the Bible generally and of the Lord Jesus in particular. I plead with you:

take to heart and believe what He says instead of defying Him for the sake of your own opinion where that opinion flies in the face of God Almighty.

And they shall go forth, and look upon the carcases of the men that have transgressed against Me: **for their worm shall not die, neither shall their fire be quenched; and they shall be an abhorring unto all flesh.** Isaiah 66:24.

And if your hand offend you, cut it off: it is better for you to enter into life maimed, than having two hands **to go into hell, into the fire that never shall be quenched, where their worm does not die and the fire is not quenched.**

And if your foot offend you, cut it off: it is better for you to enter halt into life, than having two feet to be cast **into hell, into the fire that never shall be quenched, where their worm does not die, and the fire is not quenched.**

And if your eye offend you, pluck it out: it is better for thee to enter into the kingdom of God with one eye, than having two eyes to be cast **into hell fire, where their worm does not die, and the fire is not quenched.** Mark 9:43-48 spoken by the Lord Jesus (referring to Isaiah 66:24)

And many of them that sleep in the dust of the earth shall awake, some to everlasting life, and some to shame [and] **everlasting contempt.** Daniel 12:2

A good tree cannot bring forth evil fruit, neither a corrupt tree bring forth good fruit.

Every tree that does not bring forth good fruit is cut down and **cast into the fire.**

Matthew 7:18-19 spoken by the Lord Jesus during the Sermon on the Mount

*And fear not them which kill the body, but are not able to kill the soul: but rather fear Him which is able to **destroy both soul and body in hell.*** Matthew 10:28 spoken by the Lord Jesus

*And whosoever speaks a word against the Son of Man, it shall be forgiven him: but whosoever speaks against the Holy Spirit, it shall **not be forgiven him, neither in this world, neither in that to come.*** Matthew 12:32 spoken by the Lord Jesus

*Serpents, generation of vipers, how can you escape **the damnation of hell?*** Matthew 23:33 spoken by the Lord Jesus

But and if that evil servant shall say in his heart, My lord delays his coming;
And shall begin to smite fellow servants, and to eat and drink with the drunken;
*The lord of that servant shall come in a day when he is not looking, and in an hour of which he is not aware, and shall cut him asunder, and appoint his portion with the hypocrites: **there shall be weeping and gnashing of teeth.*** Matthew 24:48-51 spoken by the Lord Jesus

*And cast the unprofitable servant into outer darkness: **there shall be weeping and gnashing of teeth.***
Matthew 25:30 spoken by the Lord Jesus

*Then shall He say also unto them on the left hand, "Depart from me, you cursed, **into everlasting fire, prepared for the devil and his angels:***
For I was hungry, and you gave me no food: I was thirsty, and you gave me no drink:
I was a stranger, and you did not take me in: naked, and you did not clothe me: sick, and in prison, and you did not visit me."

Then shall they also answer him, saying, "Lord, when did we see You hungry, or thirsty, or a stranger, or naked, or sick, or in prison, and did not minister unto You?"

Then shall He answer them, saying, "Verily I say unto you, Inasmuch as you did [it] not to one of the least of these, you did [it] not to Me."

And these shall go away into everlasting punishment: *but the righteous into life eternal.*

Matthew 25:41-46 spoken by the Lord Jesus

And to you who are troubled rest with us, when the Lord Jesus shall be revealed from heaven with his mighty angels, ***in flaming fire taking vengeance*** *on them that know not God, and that obey not the gospel of our Lord Jesus Christ: who shall be* ***punished with everlasting destruction*** *from the presence of the Lord, and from the glory of his power.* 2 Thessalonians 1:7-9

But the heavens and the earth, which are now, by the same word are kept in store, ***reserved unto fire against the day of judgment and perdition of ungodly men***. 2 Peter 3:7

Even as Sodom and Gomorrah, and the cities about them in like manner, giving themselves over to fornication, and going after strange flesh, are set forth for an example, suffering the ***vengeance of eternal fire.*** Jude 7

These are spots in your feasts of love, when they feast with you, feeding themselves without fear: clouds without water, carried about of winds; trees whose fruit withers, without fruit, twice dead, plucked up by the roots; raging waves of the sea, foaming out their own shame; wandering stars, to whom is ***reserved the blackness of darkness for ever.***

Enoch also, the seventh from Adam, prophesied of these, saying, Behold, the Lord comes with ten thousands of his saints to ***execute judgment upon all***, *and to convict all that are ungodly among them of all their ungodly deeds which they have ungodly committed, and of all their hard [speeches] which ungodly sinners have spoken against Him.* Jude 12-15

*And the devil that deceived them was **cast into the lake of fire and brimstone**, where the beast and the false prophet [are], and **shall be tormented day and night for ever and ever.***

And I saw a great white throne, and Him that sat on it, from Whose face the earth and the heaven fled away; and there was found no place for them.

And I saw the dead, small and great, stand before God; and the books were opened: and another book was opened, which is of life: and the dead were judged out of those things which were written in the books, according to their works.

And the sea gave up the dead which were in it; and death and hell delivered up the dead which were in them: and they were judged every man according to their works.

*And death and hell were **cast into the lake of fire.** This is the second death.*

*And whosoever was not found written in the book of life was **cast into the lake of fire.*** Revelation 20:10-15

*But the fearful, and unbelieving, and the abominable, and murderers, and whoremongers, and sorcerers, and idolaters, and all liars, **shall have their part in the lake which burns with fire and brimstone: which is the second death***. Revelation 21:8 spoken by the resurrected Lord Jesus

When God says, *"Vengeance is Mine. I will repay,"* He means exactly what He says. This particular phrasing is found in Romans 12:19, but many other passages such as Hebrews 10:30 and Deuteronomy 32:35-43 have a similar thrust. Isaiah 61:2 speaks of the *"day of vengeance of our God."* My search engine using a King James version found almost 40 verses speaking of the vengeance of God, and I did not try any synonyms to add to these results. The vengeance of God against His enemies and the enemies of His people is a major truth of the Scriptures and a major consolation of God's people under persecution. Revelation 12:11-12, 13:10.

The thoroughness of God's vengeance should give the toughest person pause, although in fact most people of this age close their eyes and ears to this truth. I know almost nothing about the body that the wicked will be given after death, but I can infer one characteristic. That body will transmit freely and continuously all kinds of grief, anguish and excruciating internal and external pain to the soul sentenced to endure the perpetual, unending vengeance of God. In that place there will be no water, no light and unendurable heat. There will be no sleep and no relief. No wonder the Lord Jesus repeated that *"there shall be weeping and gnashing of teeth."* Matthew 24:51, 25:30.

To the world this sounds cruel. Even to think about this is painful. *"I live, says the Lord God. I have no pleasure in the death of the wicked, but that the wicked turn from his way and live. Turn, turn from your evil ways, for why will you die, O house of Israel?"* Ezekiel 33:11. The call of this passage was given first to Israel in exile but reaches to all humanity. *"God . . . commands all people everywhere to repent."* Acts 17:30 ("Repent" and "turn" are synonyms in this context.)

In Revelation 5 we read of the opening of the seals of the scrolls that contain the judgments of God on sinful, unbelieving and unrepentant humanity. Jesus Christ there is portrayed as both the Lion of Judah and the Lamb of God. So when the Lord Jesus unleashes the judgments of God by opening the seals, He is acting as both Lion and Lamb. A lamb is among the mildest of all animals. So when we see the Lamb angered enough the break the seals as the beginning of the end, we can be doubly sure that there is massive provocation from earth. Nahum wrote immediately of the Assyrians but ultimately of all of unbelieving humanity, *"God is jealous, and the Lord revenges. The Lord revenges and is furious. The Lord takes vengeance on His enemies and He [reserves] wrath for His enemies."* Nahum 1:2. Then Nahum describes the Lord's use of nature as part of His wrath which may foreshadow portions of Revelation.

The world's judgment of God's wrath as wanton cruelty forgets the magnitude of our sin. God has given us so much in the bounties of nature, the minerals of the earth, our favorable atmosphere, marriage and family, and above all a Savior after the initial sin of our representatives Adam and Eve. Yet most of us misuse His blessings and in a figure of speech give God the finger in the face of His offer of mercy and forgiveness. The constant use of the names of God and of Jesus as curses verifies our observation. In the face of all this He will administer divine justice.

When our Lord Jesus spoke of "hell" in the Sermon on the Mount, He used the word "gehenna," a word used commonly for the Jerusalem garbage dump. We are familiar with smoldering fires in coal mines long after the initial explosion and also with underground fires when rubbish has been improperly buried. Ancient Jerusalem also needed to burn its garbage for reasons of public health, and the Valley of Hinnom to which "gehenna" referred was the location. New trash was regularly taken there, so the fires never went out. The spiritual analogy is that fallen angels and people who have rejected the Lord Jesus will be like toxic waste that must be incinerated to maintain the purity of the new heaven and the new earth, where righteousness will dwell. 2 Peter 3:13. Since these fallen angels and people have perpetual existence, the fire must likewise be perpetual. *"And the smoke of their torment ascends forever and ever."* Revelation 14:11.

Love for God's forgiven people requires permanent justice to those who remain rebellious against God. Heaven cannot be heaven if sin is present there. Therefore all sin and sinners must be quarantined away from heaven. Since they have everlasting existence, they must likewise suffer everlasting punishment because they never stop being rebellious and therefore keep adding to their sin even while in the Lake of Fire. The rebellion within the heart never changes, so the punishment demanded by justice never stops.

I plead with any reader to believe in the Lord Jesus and accept what He says at face value. Then admit to your own sin and ask the Lord Jesus for the grace to repent and believe. His blood as the sacrifice for sin at the Cross is the only escape from strict justice and vengeance. Trust Him with your present and future and ask Him to lead you from now on.

Santayana is widely quoted as having said that "Those who do not know history are doomed to repeat it." I would add as a corollary, "Those who do not know the judgment of God are doomed to endure it." Please believe on the Lord Jesus as He presents Himself before it is too late.

DOES GOD HAVE A SON?

Let's start simply. We speak of men and women becoming fathers and mothers when their children are born. It is perfectly possible to be an adult man or an adult woman and not be a father or a mother. I was a married man for over 3 years before I became a father physically when my son was born. In a more precise theological sense, one can backdate my first fatherhood about 9 months from my son's birth when my wife first conceived our son, thus reducing the interval from marriage to first fatherhood to about 2½ years in my own life. The distinction between personhood and adulthood on the one hand and fatherhood on the other should be clear enough.

But God was always a Father. He did not first become a Father when He created Adam and Eve. He always had a Son long before Creation. Hebrews 1 and Colossians 1:12-22 confirm this. Colossians 1:13 reads in part that *"He has delivered us from the power of darkness and has translated us into the kingdom of His dear Son . . ."* Colossians 1:17 says of the same Son, *"And He is before all things and by Him all things consist."* [as in the consistency of a cake, meaning "hold together," so that this truly implies that Jesus Christ exerts the force of gravity in addition to stating that the Son of God existed before anyone or anything else.]

In Genesis 14, Melchizedek appears with the titles "King of Righteousness" and "King of Peace." In Hebrews 7:3 this Melchizedek is said to have *"neither beginning of time nor end of days."* He was *"made like the Son of God."* So Melchizedek appeared to be human to Abraham but had then and still has eternal life. When one considers Hebrews

7 as a whole, Melchizedek appears to have been one appearance of the Son of God before He entered human flesh. Daniel 7:9 shows the Ancient of Days as judging; when we combine this with John 5 we realize that the Ancient of Days in Daniel and the Judge in John 5 are both members of the Godhead. They both have always existed. One can further confirm this by comparing the appearance of the Ancient of Days and His throne in Daniel 7 with the appearance of the risen Lord Jesus in Revelation 1. For further confirmation, consider Proverbs 8:22-36, in which the Son of God is described as having lived before Creation and having been *"set up from everlasting"* (v. 23). That passage shows the Son of God as having been active during Creation itself; this is matched by John 1:3 (*"All things were made by Him, and without Him was not anything made that was made."* The antecedent for "Him" is the living Word in John 1:1, who is Christ.) and by Colossians 1:16 (*"For by Him were all things created that are in heaven and that are in earth, visible and invisible . . ."*). So the God of Creation includes the Father, the Son and the Spirit (see Genesis 1:1-2).

Paul through the Holy Spirit in Romans 1:3 described the Gospel of God as *"concerning His Son Jesus Christ our Lord, who was made of the seed of David according to the flesh."* In this summary we learn that Jesus Christ was the Son of God, as all of the Gospels testify. Further, He had a human descent from King David, making Him the covenant son of 2 Samuel 7:12-14. Solomon was the initial imperfect son with blessings from God's covenant with David, but ultimately Jesus Christ was the perfect Son whose kingdom will never end. This meshes with Hebrews 1:8 and the teaching that His throne will endure forever.

For further amplification of the connections between Daniel 7 and Revelation, and the connection between Judge of Daniel 7 and the Judge of Revelation (and also of John 5) study the table that follows. We should remember that when one Person of the Triune God has an attribute, it can be applied to all three Persons of the Godhead. So it should not matter that the Ancient of Days appears to be the Father in Daniel 7 and the Son in Revelation. The Father can delegate His power of judgment to His Son with no substantive change.

Permit me a brief modern illustration to help explain the Trinity of Father, Son (Who became Jesus when He took human flesh) and Holy Spirit. Imagine a network of three supercomputers with identical features, all of which have mirror software for continuous updating and synchronization. On earth, we do this for data integrity and back-up. All three computers have the same software and the same data. Absent breakdown (which never occurs with God), they have identical performance characteristics. Each computer is capable of operating independently of the other two and they all operate simultaneously. The eyes in the beings near God's throne (Revelation 4:6) remind us that God sees and knows all; there are no data errors or omissions. Though there are three computers, yet they comprise one network. This illustration falls short of a full explanation of the Trinity, as does any human illustration. There is no explanation of the identical emotions and opinions in the Trinity in my network illustration. But the analogy does illustrate to a considerable extent how three Persons united in moral character, emotion and truth can function as a single God. It was this divine network, or divine triangle, that Satan tried and failed to break apart at the Temptation described in Matthew 4 and Luke 4.

With this partial explanation in mind to show how the Son and the Father can be identical and yet have distinct and simultaneous existence, let us compare by table the Ancient of Days of Daniel 7 and the counterpart of the Ancient of Days in Revelation.

TABULAR COMPARISION OF THE ANCIENT OF DAY IN DANIEL 7 AND THE LORD JESUS CHRIST IN REVELATION 1

Feature	Reference in Daniel 7	Reference in Revelation
Throne of judgment	7:9-10	4:5 (lamps of fire)
Clothing of Judge	7:9 (white as snow)	1:13 (no color stated except for gold band around chest)
Hair of Judge	7:9 (like pure wool)	1:14 (white like wool, as white as snow)
Multitude of ministering spirits	7:10 (thousands and 10 thousands)	5:11 (10 thousands and thousands)
Flame from the throne	7:9 (fiery flame, wheels of burning fire)	4:5 (lightnings, flaming lamps)
Judgment, opened books	7:10 (judgment set as we set trial dates, and book opened)	20:12-15 Judgment from newly opened books
Beast burned	7:11 (killed first, then body burned)	19:20 (Beast and False Prophet thrown into Lake of Fire)
Son's Kingdom	7:14 (all nations, no end)	1:18, 19:6, 19:15-16 (rules all nations with a rod of iron)

As Christians have greater contact with other faiths that look back to Abraham, there recently has arisen a controversy as to whether God has a Son. This echoes ancient controversies in which Christians were accused of having three gods in the centuries after the death and resurrection of Jesus Christ. Most Muslims and many Jews would take up the ancient controversy, claiming that Christian belief that Jesus Christ is God and the Son of God amounts to idolatry. A Jew who denies the deity of Messiah would claim that Christian belief violates the most basic Scripture of Judaism: *"Hear O Israel, the Lord our God, the Lord is one."* Deuteronomy 6:4. A Muslim scholar would most likely level a similar accusation.

The Old and New Testament Scriptures disagree. Consider Proverbs 30:4:

Who has ascended up into heaven, or descended?
Who has gathered the wind in his fists?
Who has bound the waters in a garment?
Who has established all the ends of the earth?
What is his name, and what is His Son's name, if you can tell?

So God does have a Son. When Solomon wrote, the Son had no human name and had not yet taken human flesh. The name of Jesus was supplied by the angel speaking to Mary (Luke 1:31) hundreds of years after the time that Proverbs 30:4 was first given. The angel added in Luke 1:32: *"He shall be called the Son of the Highest."* The title *"Son of God"* appears in Luke 1:35. This also agrees with Isaiah 7:14: *"Behold, a virgin shall conceive and bear a Son, and you shall call His name Emmanuel—God with us."* I recognize that in isolation a possible translation of the Hebrew would be "young woman" as an alternate for "virgin", but the Septuagint specifically understood the meaning to be "virgin." This Jewish translation of the Old Testament into Greek predates Christianity by about 300 years. Further, the use of the term "young woman" was appropriate because this prophecy had two fulfillments. The first was when King Ahaz had a son to continue the royal lineage of Judah. His name was Hezekiah, one of the best Kings of Judah. He appeared (the spelling of his name had altered over the centuries just as the French "Henri" becomes the English "Henry") in Jesus' genealogy in Matthew 1:9. That birth was not a virgin birth. The second fulfillment was the Virgin Birth of Jesus Christ described by Matthew and Luke.

Isaiah 7:14 is not an isolated reference to one unique Son of God, as one can see from Isaiah 9:6:

For unto us a child is born,
Unto us a Son is given
And the government shall be upon His shoulder.
And His name shall be called Wonderful, Counselor, the Mighty God,
the Everlasting Father, the Prince of Peace.

Once more the Scriptures declare that the Father has a Son equal to Himself. Consider each title of the Son carefully. The third and fourth titles can only be given to a Man equal with God. In fact Jesus' contemporaries correctly understood Him to make precisely that claim and accused the Lord Jesus of blasphemy on that basis. John 5:18. Jesus' work as Judge (also described starting in John 5:20) matches with the prophecy that *"the government shall be on His shoulder."* John 5:23 requires us to worship the Lord Jesus equally with God the Father. Jesus and His Father are equal and on the same plane; we are not near their level and are subordinate and inferior to both.

Jesus' claim to equality with His Father is supported by the Old Testament. In Psalm 2:12 we are warned and promised: *"Kiss the Son, lest He be angry, and you die in the way, when His wrath is kindled but a little. Blessed are all those who put their trust in Him."* Yet again the Son is given attributes that belong solely to God; therefore He is God. As John opens his Gospel, *"In the beginning was the Word, and the Word was with God, and the Word was God."* John 1:1.

Matthew is careful in Matthew 1:23-25 to specify that Mary alone, and not Mary and Joseph combined, gave the Lord Jesus His humanity. Luke follows suit in Luke 3:23. We already referred to Luke 1:35, which also specifies that the Holy Spirit would implant the Seed (mentioned by Paul in Galatians 3:16-19—Greek *sperma*, the appropriate term for conception). Even in Genesis 3:15 explaining the Fall of humanity, a Seed is promised to the woman (not through the man, as in conventional genealogies) Who will destroy Satan. So Luke explains in fulfillment of the Old Testament that a divine *sperma* was implanted in Mary's womb that grew to be Jesus Christ, Emmanuel and Son of God. The objectors are wrong even based on the Old Testament.

The heart of the controversy does not lie with modern Christians but rather lies between the accusers (ancient or modern) and Jesus Christ Himself. Jesus' claim in simplest form is stated in John 10:30: *"I and My Father are one."* Jesus' contemporary hearers understood the sweeping nature of His claim; they tried to stone Him for blasphemy. John 10:31. The word "again" refers back to John 8:56-59 when the Lord Jesus made a two-fold claim: (1) Abraham rejoiced to see the day of Jesus the Messiah on the earth; and (2) The Lord Jesus lived before Abraham and has personally seen Abraham. The hearers tried to stone Jesus then, but He simply passed through the maddened mob. For further detail on Jesus' claim to be one with and equal to God the Father, one can also consider John 5:17-47. From John 10:30 it is clear that the Lord Jesus made His claim of being one with His Father as compatible with Deuteronomy 6:4. In other words, there is perfect unity among the Persons of God, and yet those Persons live simultaneously and distinctly.

We can consider one other objection briefly. There are places in Scripture where others besides Jesus Christ are called "children of God" or "sons of God." Some examples are Romans 8:14, 19; Matthew 5:9; Genesis 6:2 and Job 38:7. This is a representative sample rather than an exhaustive search. In such cases the references are either to those who have spiritually become the yet imperfect children of God although originally alienated from Him at birth or to those who are angelic beings (good or evil depending on context) directly created by God. But it is clear in these cases that Jesus Christ Himself is not the reference. One point John makes about the Lord Jesus is found in the familiar John 3:16: *"For God so loved the world that He gave His only begotten Son, that whosoever believes on Him should not perish but have everlasting life."* This is a great salvation verse but it also distinguishes the Lord Jesus from God's lesser children as the *"only begotten Son."* There is no other that was conceived with *sperma* directly from God into a virgin woman as was the Lord Jesus.

The Apostle Paul distinguished between Adam and the Lord Jesus in a similar manner. *"The first Adam is from the earth, earthy; the second Adam is the Lord from heaven."* 1 Corinthians 15:47. Adam was made from the dust of the ground by God alone; Jesus the Son of God was born of a virgin and conceived with God's *sperma*. He is the unique Son of God Who originally lived in Heaven and has endured life as a human being in a fallen world. The Lord Jesus is uniquely qualified not only by perfection but by human experience to understand fallen humanity and will be the perfect and righteous Judge at the Last Judgment (John 5:22-23).

It follows from all this that Jesus of Nazareth, Whom God *"has made both Lord and Messiah (or Christ)"* (Acts 2:36), the One Who has conquered death and as a Son sits on the throne forever (Hebrews 1:8) is infinitely superior to all human beings. As the Egyptians had to bow the knee to Joseph when he was second in command to Pharaoh (Genesis 41:43), so every human being without exception will bow the knee to Jesus (Philippians 2:10). This includes all the conquerors already past and those yet to come. This includes the enemies of the Lord Jesus who crucified Him. This includes all of the great religious thinkers of the various ages, from Buddha to Zoroaster to Confucius to Spinoza to Mohammed and to any other thinker one can name. Atheists and evolutionists will likewise bow to Jesus Christ.

You too will bow to Jesus Christ. The only question is whether you will repent of your sins and bow down and worship Him now in joy or whether you will bow down for the first time after physical death in stark terror through clenched and chattering teeth at the Judgment. True worship of Jesus Christ as God now brings everlasting joy, peace and forgiveness. The unwilling acknowledgment of His superiority later will do you no good but will be a prelude to your everlasting judgment. The responsibility is yours. Please do not brush this issue aside as unimportant or as a mere detail, as is the modern fashion. Please also take note that the wrath of God is not a temporary condition but one that clings forever to the unbeliever in Jesus Christ as the Son of God. The Lord Jesus Himself summarized the importance of His Sonship for your eternity: *"He who believes on the Son has everlasting life; he who does not believe the Son will not see life, but the wrath of God abides on him."* John 3:36.

A FEW ACCOMPLISHMENTS OF JESUS CHRIST AT THE CROSS & RESURRECTION

So what did the Lord Jesus accomplish at the Cross? If you or I had been present, we would probably have concluded that His life was over and His cause was lost. That is what His disciples thought. They were hiding in the Upper Room, probably hoping to escape arrest by leaving with the throngs when the Passover holidays were over. The women who ventured out on the third day after the Crucifixion were carrying embalming spices, expecting to find a corpse. The two disciples who walked the Emmaus road were disconsolate in their belief that Jesus was dead. If it is the decree of God that the Lord Jesus will rule the earth, why was the Cross necessary? Why not have the Lord Jesus overthrow the Roman Empire and other contemporary governments by force and impose His direct rule? The Book of Revelation, written later, makes it clear that some day He will do just that. Why did He not just do it when He came to earth in a human body? Wouldn't the entire process have been less painful and less complicated?

I do not think that any one fallible person such as myself could detail all that the Lord Jesus accomplished at the Cross and the Resurrection. The effects are too immense for us to take in fully in our mortal bodies and fallible minds. I will try to give some idea of what our Lord Jesus did in terms of the conflict with Satan. As I sketch this, please remind yourselves that Satan fights with no holds barred, with figurative eye-gouging, biting and all sorts of brutality. In addition lies and deception are Satan's native language. And Satan is subtle. At times he will try salesmanship and seduction in place of or in addition to force. Satan's objective is no less than the overthrow of God from control of the universe. This conflict is for keeps. Then let us return to examine what Jesus Christ won at the Cross and the Resurrection.

Permit me to take the last question first. The Lord Jesus did not come to earth for Himself. Instead, He came *"not to be served but to serve and to give His life a ransom for many."* Matthew 20:28. The purpose of establishing His worldwide rule is for love, not to satisfy any lust for power. This makes the Lord Jesus unlike anyone who has sought world rule, such as Napoleon, Hitler or Stalin. Christ's bride, the true Church, has no single country and does not of itself use force, unlike any political conqueror. But Christ must rule us for our own good because of our sin. Out of love for us He seizes power that is rightfully His in the first place from Satan and from any worldly ruler who may exist for the moment.

To understand we must briefly revisit the Garden of Eden and Genesis 3, where death obtained a stranglehold on the entire human race. Both Adam and Eve followed Satan rather than God. While their bodies lived on, spiritually they died that day because they lost their ability to fellowship with God face to face. They tried to hide their nakedness with fig leaves. God gave them a real though temporary covering by killing an animal. But they were cast out of Eden and no longer had free and unhindered communication with God. Their descendants were made in their image and had the same fundamental disabilities of physical mortality and limited communication with God.

We should be thankful that God was not satisfied to leave matters as they stood. God's plan all along was to restore full sinless unity between human beings whom He had created and Himself. (The very word "atonement" in English is a constructed word from "at onement.") So God started with prayer (Genesis 4:26) and in every generation showed grace to someone. Before the Flood it was Noah. Then you can trace the growing revelation of God's grace and also His strict holiness through Abraham, Isaac, Jacob, Moses, the judges, David, Solomon and His prophets after Solomon all the way to John the Baptist. This is recorded in the Old Testament and in the beginning of the Gospels that deal with John the Baptist. But none of these could satisfy the justice of God nor erase the taint of the sins of Adam nor of the individual's unique, personal sins. Having inherited Adam's nature, even the greatest follower of God not only had his or her unique variation of Adam's sinful nature but added sinful thoughts, attitudes, actions and failures to act to their own sin nature. Just as nobody else was worthy to open the sealed book in Revelation 5:3-4, nobody was able to save himself or herself, let alone any portion of the human race, from sin and death.

Enter Jesus of Nazareth from heaven. He was born of the Virgin Mary, who was impregnated by the Holy Spirit as Matthew explained for us in Matthew 1:16-23. With no human father, He had no sin nature but He did have a complete human nature from His mother. He felt every temptation that we feel except that He had no internal sin. Hebrews 4:15. Beyond this, He actually endured the helplessness of babyhood, the frustrations of siblings and even of parents who did not understand Him, physical weakness, hunger, thirst, weariness from stress and physical labor and any other temptation that can be imagined. As related in Matthew 4 and Luke 4, He even endured temptation by Satan in person after neither eating nor drinking for 40 days and nights. Satan also tempted Him through His own disciples. Amazingly, the Lord Jesus never sinned—not even once. He loved His Father in heaven with His whole heart, soul, mind and strength! With His repeated victories over Satan before the Cross, we can begin to see how the Cross might be the start of His greatest victory of all before His Second Coming.

We sometimes say that someone who can endure something awful can endure anything. If the Son of God could endure the human death of a criminal while being scorned by infinitely inferior men, we could say legitimately that He could endure anything. The time starting after Judas left the Last Supper to betray Him through the early hours of the morning of the following first day of the week would be the acid test of whether the Lord Jesus could both

Overpower and doom Satan, as God had said would occur in Genesis 3:15; and

Undergo without sin a punishment so rigorous that it would satisfy the wrath of God against sin for all of God's people of every era (for example, consider Isaiah 53).

Many previous sharp skirmishes between God and Satan had been fought. Job was one. The struggle over the corpse of Moses was another (Jude 9). A third was recorded when Daniel was the focus of spiritual warfare between God's obedient angels and evil spirits (Daniel 8:18-27 and again in Daniel 10:12-21). But this struggle between the Lord Jesus and Satan would be the climax.

I cannot completely answer the question why God has permitted recurring evil to play out through human history instead of putting an end to all evil before now. That is something He has kept to Himself. But I can say that more people have come to true faith and will be in heaven. Jesus Christ will have His Bride, as expressed in Ephesians 5:22-33 and in Revelation 19. I also know that the time spent has resulting in the partial regathering of Israel into the Holy Land promised originally to Abraham, Isaac and Jacob and again to Moses and Joshua. That is the start of a process of the deliverance of Israel as an entire people as described in Romans 11:13-36. God waited over 400 years from the first promise to Abraham to the actual possession of the land by Abraham's posterity through Jacob. In that time the sin of the seven nations originally occupying the land became complete and their societies became fully ripe for destructive judgment. So the various societies of the world are becoming ripe today. Since none of us have the power of judgment, we cannot know the precise time. We can see the storm clouds gathering and suspect that the time is close.

Our Lord Jesus cast Satan out of heaven; no longer could Satan repeat his slanderous accusations to God about modern believers as he did with Job. Our Lord foresaw this when He said, *"I beheld Satan fall as lightning."* Luke 10:18. It is reasonable to understand this as Satan no longer having any entry to heaven but to be confined to the earth and its atmosphere. Similarly, Revelation 12:9 says, *"And the great dragon was cast out, that old serpent, call the Devil and Satan, which deceives the whole world, he was cast out into the earth, and his angels were cast out with him."* With the risen Jesus Christ now in heaven at the Father's right hand, having shed His blood for all believers and ever living to intercede for them (Romans 8:34), it is impossible to imagine how Satan would under present conditions be able to accuse any believer before God face to face. So Satan is doubly frustrated and furious in that he can no longer attack Jesus Christ directly as a man and cannot accuse His people either in the face of the saving blood of Christ. Satan is now shut out of heaven as a foretaste of being shut into the Lake of Fire to burn forever. As a blessed by-product we have the Spirit as the down payment on our complete redemption and completed salvation. We also have the means to resist the devil through humility before God. James 4:7.

The Lord Jesus accomplished the destruction of death; by His death He pioneered a road right through death to heaven for all of His people. Death at one time was Satan's stronghold (Hebrews 2:14), but now the Lord Jesus has the keys (Revelation 1:18). Satan has been ousted from his former fortress. Now all believers can pass in peace through that place that used to be terrifying, with Jesus Christ guarding each believer all the way. To recycle Mao's old phrase to a better use, for the Christian death is a paper tiger. *"O death, where is your sting? O grave, where is your victory? The sting of death is sin, and the strength of sin is the Law. But thanks be to God Who gives us the victory through our Lord Jesus Christ."* 1 Corinthians 15:55-57.

At the Cross our Lord Jesus also earned the right to open the seals of the scroll in heaven as described in Revelation 5. In particular Revelation 5:9 connects the Cross with the authority of the Lord Jesus to open the scroll. So the Cross and the Resurrection were necessary precursors to the Last Judgment that unrolls as the seals are opened. Then Revelation 6 gives the first overview of the Judgment to come.

What we could not earn, the Lord Jesus as the perfect Son of Man could and did earn from His Father. After describing the humiliation of the Cross, Paul wrote of Jesus that *"God has given Him a name that is above every name, that at the name of Jesus every knee shall bow; in heaven, in earth or under the earth; and every tongue shall confess that Jesus Christ is Lord, to the glory of God the Father."* Philippians 2:9-11. So Jesus Christ earned universal recognition from even His most stubborn enemies. I do not imagine that Satan looks like the red devil with horns which symbolizes Satan in cartoons. Whatever he looks like, through clenched teeth he will both kneel or even prostrate himself before Jesus Christ and confess that He is Lord before being consigned to his final doom. So will every person who does not believe, from famous to obscure. We may be familiar with the commercial that says that the time for gray hair is over. It would be more accurate to say that the time for sin is over, at least outside the Lake of Fire where sin will be punished forever. Jesus Christ and His people will finally be free not only from the penalty of sin, but also from its former power and from even its presence. Hallelujah!

WHO CAN ENTER HEAVEN?

"Lord, who shall abide in Your tabernacle? Who shall dwell in Your holy hill? He that walks uprightly and works righteousness and speaks the truth in his heart. Psalm 15:1-2.

We have said many times that one cannot even begin to earn heaven. But some will twist this truth to claim that it makes no difference how we behave. Ancient Greeks used to have the idea that what one does or does not do in the body makes no difference to the health of the soul. This was never the teaching of the Old Testament. All of Psalm 15 is enough to make clear that our conduct does matter. Certainly David experienced that what he did in his body made a great deal of difference as whether his soul was blessed or punished (not eternal punishment, but severe corrective punishment). His obedience or disobedience to God made a great difference as to his physical health and emotions, whether he felt joy or sadness and whether he felt close to God or estranged from Him. Abraham and especially David knew that the child of God can and must return to Him after a season of emotional separation from Him because of our holding on to our own ways or to one or more particular sins that we like. There are several Scriptures that warn humanity that certain types of people are barred forever from heaven.

This does not mean that having committed one sin of the forbidden types will bar you from heaven, but it does mean that if your fundamental character is described in such verses that you are not right with God and need to ask Him to change you immediately before your time for repentance runs out. Otherwise your ongoing sins will doom you to everlasting damnation. Let us then consider some of the verses:

Don't you know that the unrighteous shall not inherit the kingdom of God? Do not be deceived: neither fornicators, nor idolaters, nor adulterers, nor effeminate, nor abusers of themselves with mankind, nor thieves, nor covetous, nor drunkards, nor revilers, nor extortioners, shall inherit the kingdom of God.

And such were some of you: but you are washed, but you are sanctified, but you are justified in the name of the Lord Jesus, and by the Spirit of our God. 1 Corinthians 6:9-11.

The Holy Spirit blacklists people clinging to a variety of sins, including sexual sins of all sorts that violate the principle that sexual relations are to be exclusively between one man and one woman in a marriage that in principle is for life. Such sins spoil the picture that a good marriage presents of the permanent and harmonious relationship between Jesus Christ and His people, now constituted as His Church. There are also sins against the exclusive worship of the one true God. There is one sin against sobriety. There are two sins against property: one physical and one mental. If one were to review the Sermon on the Mount in Matthew 5, one would realize that at least in desire and thought every human being other than Jesus Christ has violated this list.

But this passage focuses mostly on actual behavior, and offers hope of deliverance and cleansing along with the solemn warning. Notice the change in the tense of the verbs in verse 11: *"such **were** some of you, but you **are** washed, but you **are** sanctified . . ."* Some Christians used to be some of the worst scoundrels in the whole wide world. I personally have met a men who once was an offender against at least one child who has been changed wonderfully by the Lord Jesus. There are several credible stories of convicted murderers who repented of their sins and were changed characters after their conversions to Jesus Christ. The Apostle Paul is an example of a conversion of Biblical proportions. But there is no true conversion and acceptance by God without subsequent change in the old character and the old behavior. As a general rule, the older the convert, the more drastic the change. For a fictional example, think of Scrooge in Dickens' <u>A Christmas Carol</u> when he changed from stingy to generous.

Consider another similar passage:

Now the works of the flesh are manifest, which are; Adultery, fornication, uncleanness, lasciviousness, idolatry, witchcraft, hatred, wrangling (KJV variance), *jealousy* (KJV emulations—the Greek word is for zeal and depending on context can imply either good or evil as in this case), *wrath, strife, seditions* (alternatively dissensions), *heresies, envyings, murders, drunkenness, revelry, and such like: of the which I tell you before, as I have also told in time past,* **that they which do such things shall not inherit the kingdom of God.** Galatians 5:19-21 (my emphasis for clarity's sake. I have modernized some words based on Strong's Concordance.)

Like the list in 1 Corinthians 6:9-11, sexual sins head this list. This should be a warning to the modern world, but there is practically no disposition to heed it. One difference in this list is that there is a greater emphasis on sins against love outside the sexual context, such as sins involving hatred, self-will or argumentativeness. These sins often lead to sins against truth, such as heresies.

Neither do party animals escape. Revelry and drunkenness (or use of other drugs besides alcohol) seem to go together. Most college students indulge their lusts every weekend when school is in session. Anyone who has been on a college campus after reunions can testify from the smell alone that the alumni often indulge as heartily as the students. And this is not new. Daniel 5 records the deadly results of revelry by the Babylonians as the Media-Persian coalition was hammering at the gates of the capital. (For further detail, one can consult chapter 9 of my previous book <u>Daniel's Fight and Ours</u>, Trafford Press, 2012.) The Persians caught the Babylonians revelers drunk and killed the King.

What would you say if Jesus Christ at His return caught you drunk or high?

Sins against true worship also receive attention. Idolatry, witchcraft and heresies are all mentioned. It is inconsistent to claim to believe in God and to worship Him and yet practice false worship of God or worship directed to false gods. Ezekiel 8 introduces a similar theme that continues through Ezekiel 11. Heresies—false doctrines, particularly about Jesus Christ and salvation—are the intellectual part of such sins, and idolatry and witchcraft engage the emotions in false worship. The Bible commands us to worship God with all of our heart, soul, mind and strength. Mark 12:30; Luke 10:27.

One should consider texts first from from Colossians 3:5-6 and then from Ephesians 5:5:

Mortify therefore your members which are upon the earth; fornication, uncleanness, inordinate affection, evil concupiscence, and covetousness, which is idolatry:

For which things' sake the wrath of God comes on the children of disobedience.

For you know this, that no whoremonger, nor unclean person, nor covetous man, who is an idolator, has any inheritance in the kingdom of Christ and of God.

Like the first two passages, sexual sins of the mind and body are prominent here, although covetousness is also forbidden. These lists have no particular reference to same-sex relations; it is not necessary to engage in same-sex relationships in order to displease God (but same-sex practices are denounced specifically in Romans 1:26-27). "Mortify" means to put to death and applies both to the imaginations of the mind and the practices of the body. Covetousness (which goes together with idolatry in that wanting something or someone more than God makes the object of one's desire an idol) has a very broad meaning when one refers back to the full breadth of the Tenth Commandment in Exodus 20:17:

You shalt not covet your neighbor's house. You shalt not covet your neighbor's wife, nor his manservant, nor his maidservant, nor his ox, nor his ass, nor anything that belongs to your neighbor.

In today's world we would be dealing with automobiles and pick-up trucks instead of draft animals and machines in the place of servants for most work, but the principle is as vital now as when it was first recorded by Moses. If one thinks of desiring servants for sexual intimacy instead of for work, then we would think of employees and staff members instead of old-fashioned servants that might appear in Pride and Prejudice. Either way, God is telling us in no uncertain terms with respect to anything or anyone belonging to our neighbor: Hands off! Be thankful for what God has given you. If you need more, pray and acquire it legitimately. So covetousness in Colossians 3:5-6 takes its place alongside sexual sins as forbidden. In addition, those who remain characterized by such things will be condemned to everlasting fire.

Malachi 3:5 contains a similar warning:

And I will come near to you to judgment; and I will be a swift witness against the sorcerers, and against the adulterers, and against false swearers, and against those that oppress the hireling in wages, the widow, and the fatherless, and that turn aside the stranger, and fear not me, says the LORD of Hosts.

In the immediate context of the judgment, Revelation also has its lists of people who will be forever barred from heaven and consigned to the everlasting flames. Consider Revelation 21:8 and Revelation 22:15:

But the fearful, and unbelieving, and the abominable, and murderers, and whoremongers, and sorcerers, and idolaters, and all liars, shall have their part in the lake which burns with fire and brimstone: which is the second death.

For outside are dogs, and sorcerers, and whoremongers, and murderers, and idolaters, and whosoever loves and makes a lie.

In Revelation 21:8, the paralyzing fear that is the enemy of faith heads the list of traits that will bar one from heaven. *"Without faith it is impossible to please [Him]."* Hebrews 11:6. One must either believe that Jesus Christ is the Son of God as He claimed or be judged forever by Him for one's unbelief.

Both verses are quite similar in other respects. "Abominable" can apply to many varieties of sin, and the remaining sins cover the waterfront of evil behavior, from murder to false worship. Both verses emphasize the evil of lying. Since Jesus Christ is the Way, the Truth and the Life (John 14:6), one should expect that lying would be especially offensive to Him just as false worship and murder are offensive. Our Lord Jesus demands that not only our outward behavior but our inner character conform to His.

If one were looking for a single comprehensive list of sins particularly offensive to the Holy God, one would probably start for context with Romans 1:16-17, where faith is the launching point of all holiness. In Romans 1:18 humanity is accused by God of suppressing truth that the human conscience knows in seminal form. From that suppression of truth, which triggers the denial of any impulse toward true faith, comes all sorts of horrible sin degrading both mind and body. This section continues all the way to Romans 3:20.

The Apostle Paul points out that denying that God is the Creator of humanity leads to darkening of the mind, which contaminates the conscience and results in various forms of sin of the body, including sexual sins of various kinds. We observe this in contemporary life. In my own lifetime as a part of the Baby Boom I have lived during a time when marriages often lasted for 50 years or longer (my own parents' marriage lasted nearly 68 years until the death of my father) into a time of rampant divorce into a time when many argue that there is no such thing as sexual sin among consenting adults. I have seen murders explode without even accounting for the rise of abortion. It has become natural for killers to reason that murder is not really serious because one is only killing fellow animals. The decedents are not seen as having been created by God. Suicide becomes thinkable by the same defective reasoning; if I have not been created by God, my death makes no more difference than the death of someone I might have killed.

Deceit has no divine restraint in such thinking. The fear of God would be much more effective than the Securities Exchange Commission in suppressing financial deceit in the marketplace. Since *"there is no fear of God before their eyes"* (Romans 3:18), our financial markets have become paper jungles to the point where the existence of honest capitalism is in question. Even the state government of Illinois has had to accept a settlement with the SEC for securities fraud. The rule of tooth and claw has largely displaced the Law of Love and the principles of honesty in human relations, whether among nations, within families or in markets. All this and yet more evil stems from unbelief as argued by the Apostle Paul through the Holy Spirit almost 2000 years ago.

I have tried to summarize and apply the truth of Romans 1:16-3:18 to current conditions, but my writing is no substitute for close study of the passage word by word and phrase by phrase. I would lose focus on my subject if I tried that analysis in this book. If you desire more help with that, I would recommend looking at commentaries on Romans by either Haldane or Hodge. But we cannot forget that human nature is so evil as to take pleasure in those who flaunt their sin. Romans 1:32. No wonder that in the absence of repentance the Holy One bars such people from heaven and consigns them with the Devil to the burning flames forever!

HOW CLOSE MIGHT
UNIVERSAL JUDGMENT BE?

Matthew 24:12 says, *"And because iniquity shall abound, the love of many will grow cold."* The word "iniquity" can also be translated as lawlessness. One way to try to measure lawlessness is to observe the extent to which the Ten Commandments are violated and disregarded totally. The Ten Commandments are a summary of the Law of God. Also, love is the object of the Law (Luke 10:25-37). Our Lord tells us that at the time of the end love will decline also. Love and obedience to God's Law rightly understood go hand in hand. Instead, lawlessness will increase near the time of the end.

In my previous volume, <u>Assault on Marriage: A Christian's Response</u> (published by Trafford Press, 2012), at pages 129-136, I analyzed briefly Matthew 24 and 2 Timothy 3 concerning predominant characteristics of people immdiately before the end of the age and the bodily return of Jesus Christ. The best way for any reader to assess whether or not our world may be ripe for judgment is to read these passages carefully and then compare the world around us to the predicted conditions at the end. You should not merely accept my analysis that present conditions show that the earth is nearly ripe for judgment (Revelation 14:15-19). I plead with you to read these passages for yourself and then compare the world as we now see it compared to the world described there. Consider how many of the conditions mentioned are present and how many are yet missing, and also consider whether the conditions pointing to judgment are stronger or weaker than in the previous generations. You can also consider how close world society is coming to the conditions that prevailed in previous societies which were judged, for example:

1. The world before the Flood;
2. Sodom and Gomorrah;
3. The Northern Kingdom before the Assyrian conquest (consult many of the Shorter Prophets—they are not minor—and the books of 1 & 2 Kings and 1 & 2 Chronicles);
4. Judah and Jerusalem before the conquest by Babylon (especially Jeremiah and Habakkuk and many other prophets and 1 & 2 Kings and 1 & 2 Chronicles);
5. Assyria before its conquest by Babylon, as described in Nahum;
6. Babylon in Daniel 5 before the conquest by Darius and Cyrus; and
7. Jerusalem and Judah from the time of Jesus the Messiah until the destruction in the Jewish War approximately 40 years after the Crucifixion.

The fulcrum of my presentation is that God does not change in His character (Malachi 3:6, Hebrews 13:8). Conditions that provoked Him to judgment of past societies and of their populations will provoke Him to judgment today or tomorrow. This is especially true when history and the completed Scriptures have given our generations full and fair warning of past judgments as signposts to the future universal judgment to come.

One basic test is given in Daniel 12:3-4, where Daniel gives two simple indicators of being close to the time of universal judgment: increase in knowledge and increase in travel. These prophecies are observations of the future which is now here, but they do not of themselves imply an increase in sin. They do imply an increase in the ability of a sinful leader to spread sin ande dictatorship. Imagine a Hitler or a Stalin with modern computers in place of index card files and weapons such as an H-bomb in place of crude tanks. The exponential explosion of travel and knowledge is undeniable. A century ago there was no knowledge of the human genome. Computers were unknown. Air travel did not yet exist.

We should also test how close we may be to God's coming judgment by testing current spiritual conditions against the Ten Commandments. I will be brief to keep focus on the end of days; for an extended exposition of the Ten Commandments, I would recommend the classic by Thomas Watson.

"I am the Lord your God, Who has brought you out of the land of Egypt, out of the house of bondage. You shall have no other gods before Me." This First Commandment has a positive and negative aspect. The positive aspect is that we are to worship God. As He brought the Exodus generation of national Israel out of physical slavery, so He has brought every believer out of spiritual slavery to sin and the sin nature. (John 8:31-36) Therefore we are to worship Him and be His servants as we were formerly the servants of sin and Satan. Every believer can testify that the Lord Jesus is a good and kind Master (Matthew 11:28-30) whereas Satan is unspeakably cruel, like Pharaoh but far worse. Romans 6:17-23 has the same idea.

In theory, a requirement to worship the Lord as God by itself does not necessarily exclude the worship of other gods alongside the God of Israel, as was sometimes attempted in Old Testament times. Syncretism has recurred around the world, from the ancient Greeks to the Hoa Hao in Vietnam. But our God is jealous as a marriage partner should be jealous, and such divided worship is disallowed: *"You shall have no other gods before Me."* To worship another god is to cheat on the true God in the same way that some people cheat in their marriages. It is offensive and odious. The Lord God is our only God, composed of Three Persons: Father, Son and Holy Spirit. Not only must we worship Him, we must worship Him exclusively and none other. How many people make any serious attempt to obey this?

The Second Commandment forbids the use of any images in worship. *"You shall not make for youselves any graven image or any likeness of anything in heaven above, or in earth beneath, or in the water under the earth. You shall not bow down to them nor serve them . . . "* We associate worship of images with Old Testament times, but it is still an issue in many part of the world today. One of the drivers in <u>Ice Road Truckers</u> transported a freshly made image along a perilous mountain road in India for worship by villagers there. This was to replace a similar image that was wearing out. But this command does not stop there. Because God is the Creator of all things and of all people, we cannot give any created being glory but must rather give glory to God and to God alone. For example, consider how God struck Herod dead when Herod received worship as a god (Acts 12:20-23). While certain aspects of His character are revealed in nature, the picture nature paints of God (see Romans 1:19-20 for its impression on the conscience) falls so short of His complete character that no image nor any person can be used even as an aid to our worship. Instead, we must form our mental portrait of God from the Scriptures first and secondarily from His dealings with us personally. We can and should listen to the witness of others, but we must check such witness constantly against the Scriptures instead of accepting such testimonies without verification of their principles from Scripture. This the noble Bereans did (Acts 17:11). How prevalent is idolatry in present society toward entertainers and sports figures? What about the recent proclamation of President Obama as Messiah at a celebration when the President was absent? How much idolatry of the traditional kind persists?

As a whole the picture is bleak around the globe. One cannot doubt that conditions within the Christian church are deteriorating in the United States. There is a strong underground church in China and an influential church in South Korea. North Korea has some of the most devoted Christians in the world, mostly in their prison camps. Nigeria and Latin America are experiencing spiritual harvests. There are probably underground churches in places we cannot know. But on the whole, the Bible has less influence on world societies than at any time in recent memory. This was true of ancient Israel and of ancient Judah also before their judgments. While we cannot measure with scientific precision, it is reasonable to believe that most of the world's population is becoming ripe for judgment.

The Third Commandment forbids taking the name of the Lord in vain. One common way this is breached is by using His name as a curseword. If I had a penny for every time this was voiced over a period of 1 year, I probably would have more money than a lottery winner. When I was a child, this was never heard on television. Now it is common. Certainly in common speech the names of God and of Jesus are used regularly as curses. In the United States a crucifix placed in urine has been subsidized as a work of art. That is probably a more vile curse than the usual verbal type. People who seek to use the name of the Lord Jesus with reverence at a public event are regularly challenged in court. All of this stretches God's patience with us as people and as societies and nations a little bit farther, and eventually He will respond in judgment rather than perpetual patience. I cannot say when that will take place, but it will. Of the Amorites God told Abram that *"the iniquity of the Amorites is not yet full."* Genesis 15:16. But Abram (renamed Abraham) was soon to learn that the iniquity of Sodom and Gomorrah was brim-full. Abraham witnessed from a distance God rain down fire and brimstone on the entire region, although not on the Amorites as a whole. Their judgment came roughly 400 years later during the time of Joshua, when their iniquity had become full. As measured by the curses in this world, the iniquity of this present world is filling up fast.

There is major controversy over the meaning of the Fourth Commandment. (*"Remember the sabbath day to keep it holy."*) Some, such as Orthodox Jews, still hold not only to the seventh day of the week (which beyond doubt was the original sabbath) but seek to follow the ancient rabbinical traditions concerning its observance. Some Christians also observe the sabbath on what we call Saturday. I personally have no trouble with that as an option. If I were in Jerusalem, I would probably recommend Saturday worship to a Christian church seeking to spread the Gospel to Orthodox Jewish people. The Apostle Paul met by the river in Philippi on the seventh day of the week with women of prayer (Acts 16:13). But viewing the Apostle Paul's practices as a precedent, the seventh day is no longer an obligatory worship day. Paul worshipped on the first day of the week—celebrating the Resurrection and fulfilling the 8th day of the great feasts—in Troas (Acts 20:7) and in Corinth (1 Corinthians 16:1-2). *"The sabbath was made for man, not mon for the sabbath."* (Mark 2:27, spoken by the Lord Jesus Himself) The sabbath was designed for our needed rest because of the mortality of our bodies as well as a day for worship. It was never intended as a heavy burden that it became by tradition. But how much wholehearted worship now takes place on either Saturday or Sunday? Once again I have no precise way to measure, but we do not see much public worship in modern times. As late as D-Day in World War 2, American churches were full as soon as people heard of the Normandy invasion. There was a muted reaction after September 11, 2001, but that has not lasted. Most people in the developed world think of Sunday as a shopping day instead of a worship day. This is often true of Saturday also.

When we think of the weekend, it is ironic that it was the Puritan Christian Oliver Cromwell who invented it as a way to balance work and family responsibility. In this culture, 5 days were devoted to earning a living or running a household. One day was devoted to household maintenance and projects and family entertainment. The seventh (whether Saturday or Sunday) was the day for public worship of God. How many people today in developed societies spend any appreciable amount of time on any day of the week to worship Almighty God? This lack of worship is a grave violation of the Fourth Commandment.

According to Hebrews 4:9-11, the modern analogy to the ancient sabbath is the rest of faith in Jesus the Messiah. We know that we cannot run our own lives and therefore trust Him to give us orders. With those orders He also gives peace and spiritual rest, so that we know that we can earn nothing related to salvation from God. Instead, we trust Him to give what He promised. That is the ultimate observance of the sabbath commandment.

In our assessment of how ripe our present society may appear for judgment, the Fifth Commandment concerning honoring father and mother is especially important because Holy Scripture links the widespread violation of this commandment with the nearness of the Last Judgment. One of the conditions associated with the Last Days in 2 Timothy 3:1-2 is widespread disobedience to parents. When the Lord Jesus sent out His disciples on their short mission, He addressed them in apocalyptic terms in Matthew 10, starting with verse 5. He mentions Sodom and Gomorrah as standards of judgment (10:15). In that very same discourse in verse 21 He also predicts that His own ministry will not produce peace on earth. Families will be divided. If one were to compare Matthew 10 with Matthew 24 and 25, one would find numerous similarities. The very words of the 5th Commandment (*"Honor your father and your mother, that your life may be long on the earth."*) indicate the importance of family peace to long life. For the negative side of this coin, consider Proverbs 30:17: *"The eye that mocks at his father, and despises to obey his mother, the ravens of the valley shall pick it out and the young eagles shall eat it."*

The same is true of societies. Although ancient Chinese culture had many faults when weighed by Scripture, it was noted for its strong honor within families. Although for many centuries the Chinese did not have the Biblical text which included the 5th Commandment, they nevertheless understood its importance through conscience and produced a durable culture based on the honor of parents. One of the worst effects of Maoist Communism was the destruction of the stabilizing aspects of honoring parents in ancient Chinese culture; it is no accident that the famines of the Great Leap Forward and of the Cultural Revolution followed. In general a society that does not honor parents is close to destruction. Now we see worldwide disrespect for parents and should therefore be mentally prepared for God to send judgment.

As a cross-check, consider the warnings of Matthew 24 & 25 concerning discord within families and also the portion of 1 Timothy 4 in which people will forbid to marry. Such evil practices tie in with tearing apart the family along a fault line between parents and children.

Without a stable family, it is much easier to lead the destabilized children to evil and ruin.

The history of murder is as old as Cain and Abel. This particular crime occurred before the Sixth Commandment was issued in that form. The question arises as to how we can get any idea of the nearness of the Last Judgment when murder is as old as humanity. A general answer lies in the principle stated by Jesus Christ in Matthew 24:8: *"All these things are the beginnings of birthpangs."* Have we seen an acceleration of murders in recent history? Clearly yes even though no era has been free of murder. Mass murders became far more common in the 20th century than they had been previously. The mass murders of totalitarian regimes dwarf previous experience. The Nazis, the Japanese before and during World War 2, Stalin and his henchmen, the Maoists and the Khmer Rouge practiced mass murder in unprecedented proportions to the people within reach. These tragedies dwarf the deaths cause by Ottoman inhumanity among the Armenians in 1915, which were bad enough. Add to these mass murders the tremendous number of abortions of unborn children throughout much of the known world in the latter half of the 20th century and you see a steady acceleration of the murder rate as God sees it. (For more detail on abortion as murder according to the Bible, see pp. 45-48 of my first book <u>Warnings of a Watchman,</u> Trafford Press, 2010.) Our FBI murder statistics only cover traditional murder like Cain murdering Abel. God is keeping His own count.

The Seventh Commandment forbidding theft has also long been violated. With modern computers and far-flung business enterprises, there are new opportunities for theft far beyond the traditional taking of physical property. As with murder, we see the first mass-scale Ponzi Scheme in the 20th century. Bernie Madoff took this method of theft to new depths. In the corporate world, "cooked books" have become a frequent method of theft. Enron is a 21st century paradigm. Resumes are padded routinely in a smaller variation on the same idea. Revelation 9:21 names murders and thefts as two of the four sins of which humanity will not repent even under the pressure of intensifying judgments from God. The third sin listed there is the violation of the Eighth Commandment against adultery, and usage of mind-altering drugs is the other.

Is the frequency of violation of the Eighth Commandment against adultery also accelerating in the manner of birthpangs? Cheating within marriage is far more frequent than in previous generations. Other sexual activity outside of marriage has skyrocketed among teens and older people alike. And I have not even touched on the rapidly growing acceptance of same-sex relationships throughout much of the world, not just in the United States. (For further detail on this subject, you can read pp. 55-61 of my previous book Warnings of a Watchman, Trafford Press, 2010.) Such activity has brought God's judgment in the past and there is no reason to expect anything different if it persists. Along with this is a terrible rise in the number of children who do not have their father and their mother in the same household.

The Ninth Commandment forbids false witness against one's neighbor. Moses commanded that a false witness should suffer the penalty that the witness sought to inflict on the original accused. Deuteronomy 19:18-19. The classic Old Testament case is the false evidence procured by Queen Jezebel against Naboth in order to accomplish his death and steal his vineyard, found in 1 Kings 21. We know also that the prosecutors of our Lord Jesus Christ attempted to secure false witness to put Him to death based on false testimony. Matthew 26:59-61. Although this particular plan failed, the attempt shows how far venom can drive people to claim to obey God's Law to violate it. Stephen was executed through the testimony of false witnesses. Acts 6:13. So false witness is not new.

We have no precise measure about the frequency of false witness in our present world compared to previous times, but the changed nature of our political campaigns provide a clue. In the 1950s and the early 1960s, smear campaigns were relatively rare although occasionally effective. Now smear campaigns with either spliced fragments of truth or outright lies are a regular feature of politics. A second indicator is the huge increase of office backstabbing in workplaces. If these are representative, the Ninth Commandment is another indicator of a birthpang in the form of increased disregard of the Ninth Commandment.

The Tenth Commandment forbids coveting of all kinds. *"Godliness with contentment is great gain. For we brought nothing into this world and certainly we can carry nothing out. And having food and clothing let us be content."* 1 Timothy 6:6-8. Here again there is no scientific measurement of covetousness. One of the forbidden objects of covetousness is a neighbor's wife. The increase in adultery signals an increase in the precursor sin of coveting the neighbor's wife. As to other forms of wealth, the vast increase in debt is a signal of covetousness for the things that borrowing proceeds are used to buy. Both government and private debt have exploded. In the case of private debt, bankruptcies have likewise exploded. Why? To "keep up with the Joneses." Or to buy the newest consumer items such as cars, televisions and oversized mansions in the case of those who can borrow that much. Who can forget the picture of the unfinished fortress that the jailed treasurer of Enron was building when he was arrested? It took a helicoptor to get a picture! In his case theft fueled the construction project, but foreclosures resulting from excessive debt have affected all classes from the near-poor to the very wealthy. The rise in debt is a clear signal of the rise in covetousness, which in turn is another signal that the end of this present age may be closer than most people expect.

Despite all the warning signals of the Bible, the Bible is clear that people will be caught by surprise when the judgments begin to cascade on the earth and its inhabitants. One reason is the spiritual deception which Satan will be temporarily permitted to practice, as described in Matthew 24:3,24 and in 2 Thessalonians 2:8-12. In the last passage Satan is the practitioner of the deception, but God is said to have sent it. This corresponds with the picture in Revelation of God releasing demons to perform their deadly work (Revelation 9:15). In Revelation the demons' work is military destruction and death, but it is also reasonable to believe that demons with God's permission are behind the spiritual deceit of Revelation 13 and of Matthew 24. There is precedent for this in Satan's temptation of Job, of Satan's temptation of David to order a census (compare 2 Samuel 24:1ff. with 1 Chronicles 21:1ff.) and of the Holy Spirit driving Christ Jesus into the wilderness for the express purpose of having Him face and overcome temptation by Satan himself. (Matthew 4:1, Luke 4:1) Since the people as a whole do not believe, God shall permit Satanic deception to lure the unbelievers to their final destruction as He earlier permitted one of his holy angels to be a lying spirit to Ahab's prophets (1 Kings 22:19-28) and permitted Jehu to be a persuasive liar to accomplish the destruction of the worshippers of Baal in his generation (2 Kings 10:18-28). One major reason for the surprise of the world at the judgment by Jesus Christ is the deception permitted by God as part of His plan for their destruction.

But at the same time the world is wilfully ignorant of spiritual truth. Peter prophesied (2 Peter 3:3) that *"There shall come in the last days scoffers, walking after their own lusts."* How descriptive this is of the world today! Peter then described the scoffers as denying the return of the Lord Jesus to earth and deliberately forgetting Noah's Flood. Paul more generally described that generation of refusing to believe the truth, in context of that Epistle especially the truth of the Gospel and of the return of the Lord and of right conduct (2 Thessalonians 2:8-12). The Lord Jesus spoke of misbehaving servants, apparently within a church with the label Christian, who thought that the Lord would delay His return and therefore ran riot. Matthew 24:45-51; Luke 12:42-48. The surprised servants (more precisely, ostensible servants) were consigned to the flames forever. Presence in an assembly where worship and prayer is offered to Jesus Christ of itself saves nobody. Neither does office within a church; note Paul's warning to the Ephesian elders of wolves tearing into the flock in Acts 20:27-30 accompanied by false teachers within the church. Rather, *"by grace you have been saved through faith, and that not of yourselves. It is the gift of God, not of works, lest any man should boast."* Ephesians 2:8-9.

This matches with 1 Thessalonians 5, dealing again with the fact that the world is taken by surprise by the return of the Lord Jesus to earth. The world is envisioning peace and safety when He comes for judgment. One possibility is that the world is thinking and saying "Peace and safety" because the two witnesses of Revelation 11 have just been killed. Those two men had been inflicting mini-judgments on the world, probably as a counterbalance to the Satanic false miracles and mini-miracles of the Anti-Christ and the False Prophet. Now the balance has been removed and the Anti-Christ is able to launch all-out persecution against the remaining saints on earth, thinking that there is no further retribution with the two true witnesses gone from the earth. This persecution is visualized in Revelation 13. But how wrong are the Anti-Christ and the False Prophet! Instead of fighting the two witnesses who have been killed as to their earthly bodies, they end up in combat with the resurrected Lord Jesus returning from heaven. It is absolutely no contest, and the Anti-Christ (also called the Beast) and the False Prophet are thrown alive into the Lake of Fire with brimstone, the place of ultimate torments. Revelation 19:20. By the time that the world realizes that the Lord Jesus is coming, for the wicked it is too late for anything more than vain pleas for the hills and rocks to fall on them and hide them from His wrath. Revelation 6:15-17; Matthew 24:30. The parable of the servants in Matthew 24:45-50 and in Luke 12:42-50 applies not only to false servants apparently within the Christian Church but also to the world that makes no claim to being a Christian. While the Anti-Christ and False Prophet are at their brief peak, Christianity will appear to be something to flee. But when the Lord Jesus returns, genuine Christianity trusting the Blood of Christ as the sole payment for sin and deserved damnation will be the only way to survive Judgment Day and enjoy heaven. The wrath of men—even as powerful as the Anti-Christ and the False Prophet—is fleeting and ends with the death of the body. The verdict of Jesus Christ—either *"Depart from Me, you cursed, into everlasting fire prepared for the Devil and his angels"* (Matthew 25:41) or *"Well done, good and faithful servant . . . Enter into the joy of your Lord."* (Matthew 25:21ff.)—lasts for eternity and never stops. Please for your sake repent and worship Jesus Christ while you have time!

As a quick note beyond the Ten Commandments, our Lord compared the days of Noah with the last days in Matthew 24:37. Reviewing Genesis, we find two characteristics of Noah's world: (1) Widespread violence (6:11); and (2) Continuously evil imagination (6:5). Both of these sound like our headlines, given the frequent mass murders and the explosion of pornography, to name but two characteristics of today's world. In some cases the imaginations of the heart and mind are worse than those put on screen or on the Internet. Even this is not enough; we also use drugs to intensify our evil imaginations. Revelation 9:20-21 lists this as a condition at the time of the end. Despite vast technological differences, the moral mindsets of Noah's days before the Flood and ours today are similar.

CHARACTER SKETCH— THE ANTI-CHRIST

The Bible gives us clearer information about the character of the Anti-Christ than about his appearance or national origin. Many expositors suspect that he will arise from some portion of the former Roman Empire, since the original Roman Empire was the context of Revelation. Others suspect that he will rise from the modern descendants of ancient Assyria, based on Micah 5:5 taken literally. It is clear that Micah 5:2 applies to the Messiah, the Lord Jesus. "The Assyrian" in Micah 5:5 probably does refer to the Anti-Christ, but it is fairly debatable whether the reference is to the nationality or to the character of the Anti-Christ, or both. For a description of the character of ancient Assyria, review the book of Nahum. The character of that ancient nation and its deportations of the Northern Tribes of Israel do fit the character of the Anti-Christ, regardless of his national origin. The violent character of the Assyrian Empire, especially the generation contemporary with Nahum (but not the earlier repentant generation of Jonah) fits with warlike description of the Anti-Christ in Daniel 11:36-45. (This passage appears to be an extension of the description of the warfare between the Seleucid and Ptolemaic branches of the Greek hegemony after Alexander the Great. At that time Israel became a football between them. From this passage at least one pastor has looked for the Anti-Christ to come from the descendents of the Seleucids, who were descendents of the conquering Greeks under Alexander the Great. One particular Seleucid king desecrated the Second Temple by sacrificing a sow on the altar. This was the initial "abomination of desolation" described by Daniel. But the consensus is to look back to the Roman Empire for the origins of the Anti-Christ. My advice is to keep an open mind about the national origin of the Anti-Christ.) It is absolutely clear that the Anti-Christ will be violent, although he may conceal this at first. Adolf Hitler would be a good forerunner to understand this part of the character of the Anti-Christ. Hitler waited about three years before making his first military move. This fits the warning of Jesus Christ: *"As were the days of Noah, so shall the days of the Son of Man be."* Matthew 24:37. When we refer back to Genesis 6:11 we read that *"the earth was filled with violence."*

The Anti-Christ is more than a man of extraordinary violence. He displays great diplomatic skill and conceals his violence for a time, as indicated in Daniel 9:24-27. While readings of this prophecy vary, I believe as I have written before (*Daniel's Fight and Ours,* pp. 67-80, Trafford Press 2012) that this passage has dual meanings and applies to both the First and Second Coming of Jesus Christ. I am summarizing the meaning relating to the Second Coming and the Anti-Christ's attempt to imitate and counterfeit the genuine Christ. In so doing he negotiates some form of peace treaty—perhaps a truce or a non-aggression pact—with Israel for a time of 7 years, the "week" in Daniel and previously the "week" that Jacob worked for Laban to earn his bride Rachel. Perhaps the treaty also contains security guarantees for Israel, as Germany (supposedly) guaranteed the truncated borders of Czechoslovakia after taking the Sudetenland in October 1938. In any case an Israeli government will trust this man for its security, only to face a broken covenant and war half-way through. The display of diplomatic charm will be followed by a double-cross. It would be logical to connect this double-cross with either Zechariah 9-14 or with Ezekiel 38 or perhaps both. Israel will be in a fight for her very life, having been deceived by this man through diplomatic charm.

Daniel 11:37 supplies another detail, that the Anti-Christ does not have a normal masculine desire for women. Once again Hitler is a precedent. At least one German scholar of Hitler believes that Hitler as a younger man had homosexual tendencies, and Hitler married only on the eve of his death. The text does not say that the Anti-Christ indulges in same-sex sexuality, but it leaves open the possibility that this particular man is just not interested in sex. Our Lord Jesus never married; neither did the Apostle Paul. It is quite possible that the Anti-Christ will seek to imitate the real Christ in avoiding all sexual relations and that he will have an ability to do that as part of his imitation of the real Christ.

If the Anti-Christ were alive today, we probably would not recognize him if we passed him on the street. He probably does not have the full nature of the Anti-Christ yet. Take Judas as a forerunner and example. Judas was from the beginning covetous and a thief (John 12:6), although there is no indication that any of the other disciples knew of Judas' embezzlements at the time. When one reads John's account of the Upper Room, none of the disciples recognized Judas as a potential traitor, even though he had been negotiating with the Temple rulers to sell Jesus. Like many criminals, Judas hesitated before committing his infamous crime. But when the Lord Jesus gave Judas the sop of bread, Satan took full possession of Judas (John 13:21-27). Then Judas no longer was restrained by conscience and proceeded to complete the sale of Jesus for 30 pieces of silver. The Anti-Christ will be possessed by Satan as Judas before him. But note that Judas was not possessed fully by Satan before his great crime. So I believe that the Anti-Christ will be camouflaged and unknown even to himself until the last moment when he starts on his destructive course, probably negotiating the 7-year pact with Israel mentioned in Daniel 9:24-27 as the opening act of the horrors to come.

One aspect of the character of the Anti-Christ will be his demand for worship. In imitation of the genuine Jesus Christ, the Son of God, the Anti-Christ will demand worship. In 2 Thessalonians 2:3-4, Paul prophesies that the Anti-Christ (there identified as the Man of Sin, the son of perdition) will demand worship in the Temple. (Let us set aside the question of whether this is a rebuilt literal Temple or a figure for the Christian Church as the Temple is used in Ephesians 2:21. There are also usages of the Temple in 1 Corinthians 3:16-17 & 6:19 and in 2 Corinthians 6:14-18 which might be read as the individual Christian rather than the Church as one body, but Ephesians 2:21 is clearly a corporate usage of the Temple.) For any human being other than Jesus Christ to demand worship is blasphemous. The Anti-Christ will follow suit with his master Satan, who demanded worship from Jesus Christ (Matthew 4:9; Luke 4:7). In Revelation 13 the Anti-Christ makes a like demand, also mentioned in 2 Thessalonians 2. Satan's ultimate object is to overthrow God and install his own unholy trinity of Satan himself, the Anti-Christ (also known as the Beast) and the False Prophet. Of course he will never succeed, but we should never underestimate the determination of the Devil to accomplish his abominable aims nor the havoc that his final revolts will cause. Satan will react with unprecedented rage and violence when true believers refuse to worship him. This is the root cause of all the martyrdom in Revelation.

Biblical history records several preliminary conflicts leading to the last war to come. In the days of Noah almost the entire human race joined the revolt. Only Noah's family was spared through the Flood. After that, the majority joined an efforts to build the Tower of Babel to heaven itself. God made their speech unintelligible to one another in response. Then Satan caused both of the sons of Judah to be very wicked, attempting to interfere with the Messianic ancestry of Jesus Christ. God allowed Tamar to trick Judah into perpetuating his posterity by pretending to be a prostitute to him. Athaliah attempted to kill the entire royal line of Judah when she was queen. Haman tried to kill all the Jewish people, including the Messianic line, in his plot in Persia. Herod the Great tried to kill all of the little boys of Bethlehem, but dreams to Joseph and to the magii foiled his purpose. Satan first tried to suborn Jesus in the Temptation. Then he tried to kill Jesus in order to prevent His reign, probably not anticipating that the Cross would instead inaugurate His reign. After that, Satan has been lashing out at both national Israel and at the true Church in fury because he has nothing better to try in his continued desire to overthrow God Almighty. Revelation 12 gives a panoramic view of Satan's present fury. Other portions of Revelation describe Satan's final futile efforts and his final destruction in the Lake of Fire.

A GLIMPSE OF SATANIC
REBELLION

We have already given some historical instances of human cooperation with the ongoing rebellion of Satan against God. There are two passages that give us a glimpse of how this rebellion started. In Isaiah 14, starting in verse 5, there is a denunciation of the King of Babylon. But starting in verse 14, the prophet goes beyond the King of Babylon to Satan himself, the ultimate power behind Babylon (whether here in Isaiah or later in Revelation). Paul instructs us that *"we do not wrestle against flesh and blood, but against principalities and powers, against the rulers of darkness of this world, against spiritual wickedness in high places."* Ephesians 6:12. In terms of history, we know that the rebellion of Satan started sometime after the completion of the original Creation in Genesis 1:31 and the fall of Adam and Eve into sin described in Genesis 3. We do not know how much time elapsed between the perfection expressed at the end of Genesis and the temptation of Eve and Adam. But ever since, people are faced with a choice of siding either with God or with Satan. Because, following Adam and Eve, our hearts naturally flee from God, we are by nature inclined to align with Satan despite some qualms of conscience.

Isaiah 14:12 introduces the section that extends from the King of Babylon (ugly enough) to Satan himself. It starts with the fact that Satan had fallen from heaven; this corresponds with the fact that Satan had to communicate with God specially concerning Job (Job 1:6-12; 2:1-6). Our Lord Jesus foresaw a further fall of Satan (Luke 10:18-20), which appears to correspond with Revelation 12 and the further fall of Satan recorded in 12:8-9. Finally Satan will be confined in the Lake of Fire forever (Revelation 20:10). Christ and all who follow Him do not enjoy that pleasure yet, but we will.

Returning to Isaiah 14:13-15, it is important that Satan five times starts his pretensions with "I will."

*"For you [Satan] have said in your heart, **I will** ascend into heaven; **I will** exalt my throne above the stars of God; **I will** also sit in mount of the congregation on the sides of the north; **I will** ascend above the heights of the clouds; **I will** be like the Most High. Yet <u>you will be brought down </u>to hell, to the sides of the pit."*

Thank God that Satan will never succeed in any of his boasts. If you ever need a sermon to yourself about the evils of pride, please turn back to this verse and remind yourself of how satanic pride truly is.

Ezekiel 28 uses the same basic technique of starting with an earthly king (in this case, the king of Tyre in what is now southern Lebanon) and extending to Satan, the power behind this earthly throne. Ezekiel 28:12-16 starts the description of Satan in his original unfallen state:

Son of man, take up a lamentation upon the king of Tyre, and say unto him, Thus says the Lord GOD, 'You seal up the sum, full of wisdom, and perfect in beauty. You have been in Eden the garden of God; every precious stone [was] your covering, the sardius, topaz, and the diamond, the beryl, the onyx, and the jasper, the sapphire, the emerald, and the carbuncle, and gold: the workmanship of your tabrets and of your pipes was prepared in you in the day that you were created. You [are] the anointed cherub that covers; and I have set you: you were upon the holy mountain of God; you have walked up and down in the midst of the stones of fire. You [were] perfect in your ways from the day that you were created, till iniquity was found in you. By the multitude of your merchandise they have filled the midst of you with violence, and you have sinned. Therefore I will cast you as profane out of the mountain of God; and I will destroy you, O covering cherub, from the midst of the stones of fire.'

The name "Lucifer" means "light-bearer." So Satan in his unfallen state was involved with the Light of God. He was the "anointed cherub", which would correspond to Jesus as the Anointed One, the Messiah (in Hebrew) or the Christ (in Greek). Jesus Christ was and remains the Light of the World. John 1:9. Instead of accepting his honored place in the perfect Creation next to the Son of God, Satan rebelled and has tried to either overthrow or seduce the Son of God, as in the Temptation written in Matthew 4 and Luke 4. From Satan's distorted perspective, he hoped to seduce Jesus Christ as he had earlier seduced Eve and then Adam and then use Jesus Christ to try to overthrow His Father. Of course this was a hopeless undertaking, but that did not deter Satan from trying. Now that Satan finds himself confined to the earth and its atmosphere, he will wreak all the havoc he can.

Ezekiel 28:17 gives an origin of the fall of Satan: *"Your heart was lifted up because of your beauty; your wisdom was corrupted because of your brightness."* Does not this sound modern, like many movie stars today and in the recent past? What good did beauty do for Marilyn Monroe or for Natalie Wood? Was Rock Hudson's life blessed because he was handsome? Satan was full of himself to the point where he ceased desiring to serve God. So many talented people have fallen into the same trap. The ancients were right—pride is a killer just like a heart attack. Satan is already spiritually dead and doomed to eternal damnation and perpetual punishment and pain because of pride. Medieval theologians recognized pride as one of the seven deadly sins; the ancient Greeks in their myth of Narcissus were smart enough to realize that we cannot fall in love with ourselves without killing ourselves in the end. Instead of loving our sinful selves, we must repent and ask God to start changing our sinful selves. *"What shall it profit a man if he should gain the whole world and lose his own soul? Or what shall a man give in exchange for his soul?"* Mark 8:36-37.

One may reasonably ask why Satan failed with Jesus Christ where he had succeeded with Adam and Eve. The answer lies with the differences between Adam and Eve on the one hand and Jesus Christ on the other. Following 1 Corinthians 15, I will speak of Adam alone; the characteristics of Adam and Eve were originally alike except that Adam was male and Eve female. Adam was originally sinless and immortal, without sickness or flaw. But Adam possessed free will. He had the potential to sin. As Psalm 8 celebrates, Adam was created to govern the original sinless creation of God on earth. He was "a little lower than the angels" but nevertheless had glory and honor. So did Eve. But all that was lost in the Fall, when Adam and Eve both exercised their free will to sin against their Creator. Given that Satan as an angel had once outranked Adam and Eve, we can look back and have a clue how Satan might have succeeded with his ruse of using the serpent to talk with Eve. Adam and Eve became mortal and ever conscious of their sin (meaning not only particular sins, but sin in the greater sense of perpetually falling short of God's rightful demands not only as to their actions but as to their thoughts and feelings as well).

Contrast the nature of Adam and Eve with that of Jesus Christ. As 1 Corinthians 15:47 contrasts, *"The first man is from the earth, earthy; the second Man is the Lord from heaven."* This statement echoes what the Lord Jesus said in John 6:47-51:

Truly, truly, I say unto you, He that believes on Me has everlasting life. I am that bread of life. Your fathers did eat manna in the wilderness, and are dead. This is the bread which comes down from heaven, that a man may eat of it, and not die. I am the living bread which came down from heaven: if any man eat of this bread, he shall live for ever. And the bread that I will give is my flesh, which I will give for the life of the world.

Adam was formed from the dust of the ground; the Lord Jesus came from heaven, not from earth. Adam was created as an honored subordinate to God; Jesus was equal with God (Philippians 2:5) from the very beginning. John says simply, *"In the beginning was the Word, and the Word was with God, and the Word was God."* John 1:1. So Satan in his rebellion was attempting to set the Son of God against His Father when Satan tempted Jesus. Satan sought civil war between Father and Son in order to establish his own kingdom out of the wreckage (referring back to Isaiah 14 especially). When iniquity was found in Lucifer, he had become a being who would rather rule a ruin than serve within a harmonious kingdom. This characteristic will be displayed again in Revelation, as all of the blood and gore at the end shows. But thankfully, this was an impossibility. Just as the character of the Father is unchangeable (*"I am the Lord; I do not change. Therefore you sons of Jacob are not consumed."* Malachi 3:6), so is Jesus Christ unchangeable (*"Jesus Christ the same yesterday, today and forever."* Hebrews 13:8). Our salvation through the blood of Jesus Christ and the ultimate suppression of Satan's rebellion is not contingent but is made certain by the unchanging holy and loving character of *"our great God and Savior Jesus Christ."* Titus 2:13.

SATAN'S AND THE ANTI-CHRIST'S USE OF DECEPTION

In John 8:44 our Lord Jesus characterized Satan: *"He was a murderer from the beginning and did not abide in the truth, because there is no truth in him. Whe he speaks a lie, he speaks of his own, for he is a liar and the father of it."* To get context for the Anti-Christ's use of deception during the Last Days, we can trace Satan's lies starting with the Garden of Eden. He began his deception of Eve by questioning God. *Yea, has God said . . . ?* (Genesis 3:1) By Genesis 3:4 Satan was telling an outright lie: *"You shall not surely die."* And Satan has been lying ever since. Jeremiah observed that the leopard cannot change his spots (Jeremiah 13:23); so Satan will not change his deceptive nature, although he may use that deceptive nature to appear as if he were an angel of light, as he once was. 2 Corinthians 11:14.

In Acts 5:3 Satan is displayed as the originator of the lies of Ananias and Sapphira about their land transaction. In Revelation 3:9 the synagogue of liars is shown to be under the control of Satan. And who can forget the kiss of Judas, professing love on the outside but concealing greed and betrayal of the Lord Jesus on the inside? Judas was able to play his deceptive part because earlier than evening *"Satan entered into him."* John 13:27.

Satan tried a half-truth with the Lord Jesus during the Temptation (Matthew 4; Luke 4). When he offered to Jesus the kingdoms of the world, Satan was offering to Him what had already been promised to

Jesus by His Father. For support of this, review the numerous passages in the prophet Isaiah in which the Gentiles)or nations, depending on your translation(will trust in the Messiah. Satan did have temporary sway over the nations, which was soon to be broken. Indeed he was being clever as well as desperate in offering what he was about to lose in exchange for Jesus' worship of him and the consequent rupture of the Trinity. Satan could not have kept his implied promise of permanent rule over the nations. Neither can Satan fulfill anything that he offers any human being because of the overruling sovereignty of God. For example, Satan may promise ecstasy through drugs, stolen money or adultery but instead he brings misery and even shared doom in the wake of sin. He may promise deliverance from misery through suicide but instead leads his depressed follower straight to damnation by Almighty God. Satan will follow in his turn soon enough.

With this context, we should expect to find references to Satan's deception during the Last Days. In referring to the Anti-Christ, Paul wrote in 2 Thessalonians 2:9-12 *whose coming is after the working of Satan with all power and signs and lying wonders, and with all deceivableness of unrighteousness that perish, because they did not receive the love of the truth that they might be saved. And God will send them strong delusion that they should believe a lie, that they all might be damned that did not believe the truth but had pleasure in unrighteousness."* This is a case where God will permit Satan's deception to have full sway in order to accomplish His own objectives. In effect God is turning Satan's rebellion against Satan himself by using Satan's deception as the means to kill Satan's human allies. Another instance of Satan's deceptiveness is in Matthew 24. At the very beginning of His sermon our Lord warns his disciples in verse 4 not to be deceived by anyone. In verses 23-27 He returned to this theme: *"Then if any man should say to you 'Lo, here is the Christ,' or 'there', do not believe it. For there shall arise false Christs and false prophets and shall show great signs and wonders, so much so that they would, if possible, deceive the very elect. Behold, I have told you before. Wherefore, if they should say to you 'Lo, he is in the desert,' do not go forth. 'Behold, he is in the secret chambers,' do not believe it. For as lightning comes out of the east and shines even to the west, even so shall the coming of the Son of Man be."* The genuine return of the Lord will be so earthshaking and electric that even the wicked—far too late to do them any good—will be undeceived and will try their best to run away and hide, just as Adam did in the Garden. Revelation 6:14-17. In Revelation 20:7-10, Satan after being released from restraint returns to his deceptive ways. Satan's deception will come to nought and he will burn forever.

SATAN'S ALLIES IN
HIS REBELLION

Satan in the Garden did obtain the allegiance of the majority of humanity when he suborned both Adam and Eve from their proper loyalty to God in the Garden of Eden. There are other allies also. There is good reason to suspect from Revelation 12:4 that Satan also persuaded one-third of the angels to join him in his rebellion. The usage of stars as a symbol of angels is found at least twice in the Old Testament. One is in Job 38:7, where there is a reference of "morning stars" singing for joy at the creation of the earth. Since Adam and Eve had not yet been created, the singers must be been angels. The other is in Judges 5:20: *"They fought from heaven; the stars in their courses fought against Sisera."* Stars might even be a physical representation of holy angels; in that case black holes may be where fallen angels are imprisoned)Jude 6(. But some fallen angels, also known as demons, yet move within the domain of the earth.

A brief survey of the misery caused by demons is sufficient proof of their evil. When multiple demons possessed a man in Gadara, they caused him to cut himself, to live in a graveyard and to go about naked. (Mark 5:1-5; Luke 8:27). When a demon possessed a child, that child often tried to kill himself by throwing himself into a fire or into water. (Matthew 17:15) We should probably add to this description the fact that the Devil himself is a murderer and a liar (John 8:44), thus by habit and nature violating the Seventh and Ninth Commandments. Demons can be expected to help Satan carry out his murder and deceit. Before we leave this, we should note the pain that demons cause and contrast it to the joy that the Holy Spirit gives to the believer. Consider for a moment the fruit of the Spirit starting in Galatians 5:22 and contrast them with both the deeds of the flesh starting in Galatians 5:16 and the pain that demons cause someone who is possessed. It is infinitely better to have the Holy Spirit within than to have a demon—or better stated for a demon to have you. Like earthly revolutions such as the French and Russian Revolutions, Satan consumes and discards his own people as soon as a person's usefulness as a tool is exhausted. God, by contrast, loves His own people for eternity. Obviously the two kingdoms cannot mix with any stability, and in the long run one or the other must fall. The Last Judgment completes this process.

SPECIFIC INSTANCES
OF SATAN'S SKIRMISHES
AGAINST GOD

After Adam and Eve were expelled from the Garden of Eden, we see in Genesis 6-7 that humanity became so wicked that God destroyed the entire human race except for Noah and his family. We do not know precisely how Satan exercised his influence over humanity, but there was the murder of Abel by Cain in the first generation after Adam and Eve. Polygamy and perhaps other forms of sexual immorality came shortly thereafter. Human imagination was perverted into the service of evil. Violence proliferated. So God sent the Flood to kill almost all of the human race and rebuild a new society starting with Noah and his family.

Once again it did not take long for evil to rear its head. Nimrod started the Tower of Babel to attempt to reach heaven. It is reasonable to infer that his intention)or perhaps Satan's intention(was to use the Tower as a base from which to fight God. We know that God introduced the variety of human languages to bring this building project to a halt. Then a specific conflict between God and Satan arose over Job.

Job was unusually faithful to God. Satan accused Job of selling out his loyalty in exchange for God's protection and material prosperity. In his arrogance, Satan could not imagine a human being truly loving God for His character. In one sense Job was a trial case of whether it is possible to genuinely convert a human being from his or her innate loyalty to Satan to the love of God for His own sake, as distinguished from loyalty as part of a bargain. So God in two stages permitted Satan to do anything to Job except to kill him. Having lost wealth, health and 10 children, Job writhed in both physical and emotional pain. In that state of suffering Job faced an earthly foreshadowing of the Lake of Fire with its physical and emotional pain. But Job, while imperfect, maintained his faith and remained loyal to God without God's protection. So genuine conversion from the sin nature allied to Satan to a new righteous nature allied to God is indeed possible. In another sense the temptation of Job was a foreshadowing of Satan's later attempt to tempt Christ Himself.

Another instance of Satan's efforts to interfere with the coming of the Messiah center around Judah, one of the sons of Jacob (Genesis 38). I can only assume that Satan had made a shrewd guess that from Judah would come the Messiah, because the oldest of Judah's sons were so wicked that God killed him. The next son refused to father a son in the place of his deceased older brother, so God killed him too. The third son was too young to immediately step into the place of his brothers. I suspect Judah thought that the woman was "bad news" and never intended to give his last son to the twice-widowed woman. Matters were at a standstill when the woman decided to trick Judah into thinking that she was a prostitute. He took the bait and impregnated her with twins without intending to do so. So it was Judah himself that ultimately stepped into the shoes of his sons and procreated a son for each of his dead sons, as ancient law demanded. From one of these ultimately descended Jesus of Nazareth, the Messiah. Like a cartoon villain, Satan was foiled again.

Through the Pharaoh who did not know Joseph, Jacob's most illustrious son, Satan tried to prevent Messiah from being born by instigating that Pharaoh to order all Jewish males killed. Moses was delivered from death through the stand taken by Pharaoh's daughter against the law of her own father. As later in the times of Esther, God used a courageous woman to check Satan's design. From the later history of the Exodus, we know that it was not only Moses that was delivered but the Hebrew male children generally by the courageous midwives and by Pharaoh's daughter's example.

As one proceeds down through history, another attempt by Satan to thwart the birth of Messiah occurred during the divided kingdoms when Athaliah became the <u>de facto</u> ruler of Judah (2 Kings 11—see also chapter 10 for background). After her son had killed all of his brothers in order to insure his own succession, Athaliah killed all the royal children of Judah—except one hidden by the High Priest in the Temple—in order to remove any potential challengers to her power. Through this one child came the Messiah.

A later attempt by Satan to prevent the birth of Messiah came during the Persian period portrayed by the Book of Esther. Haman's plot encompassed not only the Persian capital but the entire Persian Empire, including Jerusalem. That would have swept up Zerubbabel and his immediate descendents as well as Esther, Mordecai and her family. But God providentially kept the king awake and caused him to learn of Mordecai's unrewarded loyalty, which in turn helped Queen Esther turn the King against Haman. The Jewish people were preserved again as a minority under Gentile government.

Still another murderous attempt to prematurely kill the Messiah occurred shortly after the Lord Jesus was born, when King Herod pretended to want to worship the Messiah. God intervened by dreams to both the *magii* and to Joseph, the husband of Mary the mother of the Lord Jesus. The family fled just in time to escape Herod's troops as they killed all the male children 2 years old or younger in the area of Bethlehem. So the Lord Jesus survived to grow to adulthood, when He faced Satan in the Temptation.

Satan now made his last three desperate throws. As recorded in Luke 4 and Matthew 4, Satan tried to tempt the Lord Jesus in 3 ways after the Lord had spent 40 days without food or water. He tempted the Lord Jesus to make the stones bread to satisfy His hunger. Satan suggested that Jesus throw Himself down from the Temple in the presence of the people and in that way cause a sensation. And Satan offered all the kingdoms of the world—which already rightfully belonged to the Lord

Jesus—to Jesus if He would worship Satan. In all cases the Lord Jesus repelled the temptations with quotations from Deuteronomy.

Now Satan's last two chances were to either (1) Persuade Jesus to bypass the Cross so that there would not be a blood sacrifice to wipe away our sins; or (2) Keep Jesus dead if He did die on the Cross. Satan tried the first option through Peter when Peter resisted the concept that Jesus should die. Jesus' reply to Peter was in modern language, *"Get away from Me, Satan! You are an offense to Me. You do not savor the things of God but rather the things of men."* (Matthew 16:23) When using Peter did not work to deflect the Lord Jesus from His plan, Satan last desperate option was to prevent the Resurrection, which afforded no hope for Satan at all. Satan was doomed from the start, but Satan was so selfish that he has continued his rebellion to the very end. Since Jesus Christ Himself is now out of reach, Satan now attacks His Body, the Church and His chosen nation Israel. Revelation (especially chapters 12, 13 and 20) makes clear that Satan will never willingly stop his destructive behavior—instead he eventually will be imprisoned so as to be unable to continue but only to suffer. He will never be the ruler of the underworld. Instead he will be the arch-criminal of the underworld undergoing the most severe everlasting punishment. No sensible person wants to share any degree of his punishment.

COMPARISON BETWEEN EARTHLY CONFINEMENT AND THE LAKE OF FIRE— HOPELESS HELL

I should write a brief note on the nature of the judgment that Jesus Christ will inflict upon those to whom He says, *"Depart from Me you cursed into everlasting fire prepared for the Devil and his angels."* Matthew 25:41. In Revelation we know that *"death and hell were cast into the Lake of Fire."* Revelation 20:14. From the most cursory examination we know that the bodies of the damned are either literally on fire or they feel like it. This is among the most painful sensations known to humanity. Beyond this, we are informed that the condemned must drink in the wrath of God at full strength without dilution. Revelation 14:9-10. I do not know precisely what this means, but it suggests the internal pain which on earth might be caused by advanced cancer, arthritis, acid reflux disease, shingles and other deficiencies of the body which cause terrible pain. Another idea would be a perpetual hangover. On earth we would administer pain-killers to give relief, but in the Lake of Fire not even aspirin would be available. In Luke 16:19-31, the rich man was denied even water for his burning tongue. That was in the holding cell, not in the final place where the sentence of the second death will be perpetually endured. Then superimpose on this grim scene the nausea and internal pain of perpetually breathing in malodorous sulfur compounds generated by the brimstone that we know are present from

Revelation 20:10 and 21:8. Miserable is not nearly strong enough to describe this existence of non-stop excruciating pain.

And with my thumbnail of physical pain I have not scratched the surface of the full horrors of hellfire. The mind is as tormented as the body, without the availability of insanity or forgetfulness as a refuge. The rich man of Luke 16:19-31 in his holding cell was forced to remember the riches he had on earth. Then he had to face the misuse of his former riches and the contrast between those riches and his current state, separated from heaven with his tongue on fire as but a down payment on the full punishment to come. Imagine being forced to watch a "lowlight reel" of your own life with all of its sin, from wicked thoughts to wicked words to wicked deeds, reminding you of why you are where you are and why you will perpetually stay there. The condemned will probably be disgusted with themselves for blowing opportunities for eternal life and for leading others astray and yet remain hateful toward God for exacting the punishment that justice requires. The condemned will be selfish throughout eternity.

There is a common misconception that Satan is in charge of hell and that the punishments there are authored by Satan. This is not true. Revelation 20 contains some items not easy to understand, but at least one truth is clear: Satan does not control hell or the Lake of Fire. Instead he is the most prominent prisoner and sufferer there. In Revelation 20:3, Satan is imprisoned in the bottomless pit for 1000 years, assuming that the text is to be read literally. Even if we suspend discussion as to the meaning of the 1000 years, there is no doubt that Satan is a prisoner, not in charge of the prison. Then after Satan was set free for a short time and again captured, *the Devil that deceived them is cast into the Lake of Fire, where the Beast and False Prophet are, and shall be tormented day and night forever and ever."* (Revelation 20:10) Clearly Satan is not in charge of his own torment. Rather, payback time has begun. *"Vengeance is Mine. I will repay, says the Lord."* Romans 12:19; compare Deuteronomy 32:35-43; Psalm 58:10-11, 94:1-3, 149:5-9; Isaiah 34:8, 35:4, 63:4; Micah 5:5-15; Luke 21:22; 2 Thessalonians 1:8, Hebrews 10:30.

Then it must be God Himself Who inflicts the perpetual judgments of the Lake of Fire. To take one example, members of the Jewish leadership (already under sentence of spiritual death by the Lord Jesus pronounced in John 8:21 and reiterated in John 8:24) who persuaded Pilate to condemn Jesus Christ to crucifixion actually mocked and derided Him when He was in physical agony on the Cross. Luke 23:35-37. Psalm 2:4 prophetically gives the answer: *"He that dwells in the heavens shall laugh; the Lord shall have them in derision."* God has always lived in heaven. Does the Lord Jesus now dwell in the heavens? Indeed He does: *"God . . . has in these last day spoken to us by His Son . . . Who sat down by the right hand of the Majesty on high."* (excerpted from Hebrews 1:1-3 to focus on this question—the Scriptures omitted here for clarity are vitally important in other contexts and are worth much study, but I am focusing on one point for now). In Revelation 1-3, Jesus Christ is also shown as being in heaven, not on earth. The Ascension in Acts 1 is based on eyewitness accounts of that event. And Revelation 19:11 says this: *"And I saw heaven opened, and behold a white horse, and He that sat on it is called Faithful and True, and in righteousness He judges and makes war. His eyes were as a flame of fire* [compare this portrait with Revelation 1:13-17 if you have any doubt that Revelation 19 again is describing Jesus Christ] *and on His head were many crowns, and He had a name that no man knew but He Himself; and He was clothed with a robe dipped in blood, and His name is called the Word of God."* [compare John 1:1]. From the combined testimony of Scripture, the judgments of God are the joint action of both Father and Son, but the Son is the Judge at the Last Judgment (John 5:22-30; Matthew 25:31-46). This confirms that modern humanity must change its entire view of the Godhead from an indulgent grand-father figure to a sovereign King Who demands obedience from His created subjects and judges persistent rebels with everlasting punishment.

As I review my last paragraphs, I realize that I have passed too quickly over the words in Matthew 25:41 of our Lord Jesus, *"everlasting fire."* Paul used very similar words in reference to the wicked in 2 Thessalonians 1:9: *"who shall be punished with everlasting destruction from the presence of the Lord and from the glory of His power."* One way to get closer to the implications of these verses and others like them is to compare what we know about the Lake of Fire with some of the worst places on earth. These would be concentration camps run by various totalitarian regimes of the 20th century. Since we captured intact Nazi concentration and death camps, we probably know them best. But we have eyewitness accounts from Alexander Solzhenitsyn and Natan Shakarinsky about Soviet camps. Victor Kravchenko was a living witness from the Stalinist 1930s who escaped to the United States and published what he endured. Nora Lam lived in China during some of the worst persecutions there. And in Cambodia Dith Pran saw the concentration camps there and escaped to witness to the truth. The operator of one of the notorious Cambodian prisons, "Comrade Duch", has himself supplied considerable detail as to what occurred. The Devil's Island prison where Alfred Dreyfus was held may have been almost as bad. So even without personal experience we have a basis to compare some of the worst in human confinement with the Bible's description of the afterlife of the damned.

As I go through the comparison, it is not important whether the various items are literal or figurative equivalents. For example, I do not truly know whether the Lake of Fire has a gaseous atmosphere like that on earth or whether something unknown will create a like sensation or effect. I cannot state the precise nature of any body that the damned may have or whether the pain will be real or phantom pain analogous to the pain that an amputee may feel from the amputated limb. We cannot know the mechanism of the punishments but from the descriptions in the Bible we know their reality.

Under the very worst conditions on earth the inmates have breathable air and some water. As a contrast, the damned in the Lake of Fire have air fouled with sulfur (brimstone) compounds which would nauseate and burn the lungs. Even in Luke 16:19-31 where the rich man was in a holding cell, he was denied water and his tongue was on fire. After the Last Judgment his entire body, not just his tongue, will be on fire.

In any human prison the temperatures are kept within some habitable range although in some cases extremely uncomfortable. The guards must have endurable conditions. A reasonable guess would be a range from—30°C. to 40°C. There is at least some rudimentary clothing and shelter. To make some guess as to the possible temperatures of the Lake of Fire, the closest equivalent of which we know might be the temperature inside the sulfurous gases emitted by a volcano. From the damage to the bones at Herculaneum these have been estimated at around 500°C. There may be comparable measures from other eruptions. But the gap is so wide from our worst confinement that we have no experience comparable to it. Needless to say, there will be no liquid water at such a temperature, nor would any known clothing or shelter survive.

Human prisons have light and dark like other places, with the exception of one underground German prison in World War 1 that housed military escapees that had only artificial light. Natural scenery would be visible. There is sleep. But in the Lake of Fire there is neither rest nor sleep (Revelation 14:11). Without light, nothing and no one can be seen. There will be only the sadness and torment of *"blackness of darkness forever."* Jude 13. This statement of perpetual blackness raises an inference that the Lake of Fire may be like a superheated black hole with crushing gravity being the confining force instead of an external fence or barbed wire. Even the human skeleton (or whatever is analogous to our skeleton) will be strained perpetually to the breaking point. The resulting pain would prevent sleep—imagine crushed vertebrae and the jangling nerves of rotten teeth on fire with no relief ever as an analogy to get some idea of the awful reality.

Friendship is possible in human prisons. Except for people in solitary confinement, there are meals together. Conversation, even if with guards, is available. For a time Dith Pran and his wife remained together on a prison farm. Some Nazi prisons had occasional musical performances for the benefit of the guards that brought some variation to the prisoners' misery. But in the Lake of Fire human interaction will be impossible in pitch darkness like that of Egypt before the Exodus.

Rather than music, there shall be *"weeping and gnashing of teeth."* (Matthew 8:12; 13:42, 50; 22:13, 24:51; 25:30; Luke 13:28). I have heard people say that they would prefer to go to hell rather than to heaven because their friends will all be there. One problem with this is that their former friends will be preoccupied with themselves and their own pain even if renewed contact were somehow possible. Friendship will not survive in the Lake of Fire. Neither will any other form of enjoyment. Nothing that we now know or may endure can prepare us for the shock and awe of the Lake of Fire, nor for the pain to be endured forever. I speak not of physical pain only. I believe it was George Orwell who described the fictional tyranny of Big Brother as "a boot in your face forever." As to the psychological part of the Lake of Fire, that was a fair description. Literally and figuratively, you don't want to go there no matter how much pleasure you are deriving from blatant sin now. There just is no comparison with any misery on earth. Neither is there any comparison between any earthly trouble and heavenly reward. *"For the sufferings of this present age are not worthy to be compared to the glory that shall afterward be revealed in us."* Romans 8:18.

One appropriate nickname for the Lake of Fire could be "Hopeless Hell." On earth, even someone sentence to life without parole has the hope of clemency from the Governor and perhaps visits in the meantime. The Jews of Sobibor had enough hope to stage a mass escape with the help of a Russian captain, himself a prisoner. The Apostle Peter was delivered by an angel from a scheduled execution the following day (Acts 12). 1 Corinthians 13:14 reads, *"But now abide these three: faith, hope and love. The greatest of these is love."* In the Lake of Fire there can be no faith but rather enmity toward God. There will be no love either in the black isolation and pain. Neither will there be any hope because there is no possibility of pardon and not even a dream of escape. There will not even be illusions on which to construct a false hope, but only the black certainty of perpetual physical, mental and emotional torment without relief.

Heaven and hell are portrayed as polar opposites in Scripture. Heaven has no darkness; hell has no light. Heaven has abundant water; hell has none. Heaven is full of friendship; hell has none. God is ever-present in heaven; God is ever absent in hell although He maintains the punishment from the outside. (In a limited sense of the absence of God the atheist gets what he or she wants now, although in ignorance of the full consequences.) Jesus' enemies laughed at Him on earth (Luke 23:35); the Lord Jesus will have the last laugh at them in heaven (Psalm 2:4). Heaven will be full of music more wonderful than any on earth; hell will be full of sobbing and wailing but will have no music. In heaven there will be no pain nor grief; hell will be full of pain and grief. There will be everlasting joy in heaven (Isaiah 35:10, 51:11, 61:7) and everlasting woe in hell (Revelation 20:10-15, 21:8; 2 Thessalonians 1:8-9; Matthwe 25:46). In terms of Matthew 25, people who follow through faith the Good Shepherd like sheep will end up in heaven whereas those who serve their self-will and are disobedient like goats end up in hell. In the end permanent spiritual reality is that simple, so that a young child can understand the basic truth.

SOME THOUGHTS ON HEAVEN

We have considered the Lake of Fire. What about Heaven? Just as there are aspects of the wrath of God that we cannot now understand, there are also aspects of Heaven that we cannot imagine. Isaiah 64:4, 1 Corinthians 2:9. It is not the current Heaven which we can glimpse in Revelation, but there will be a new heaven and a new earth, in which righteousness will dwell. 2 Peter 3:13. But we have some clues about the nature of heaven. As a counterpoise to the previous consideration of the Lake of Fire, we will pursue what we can. We should consider what it means to *"enter into the joy of your Lord."*

To start, we will have a spiritual body different from the body we now have (1 Corinthians 15:35-49). Our current body is subject to fatigue and death, but our new bodies will be free from any such thing. Our current bodies are divided by gender, but the new body will be like the angels and not have gender. Mark 12:25. Marriage will no longer be necessary. Our current bodies are subject to gravity. Since our new body will be like the new body of the Lord Jesus (Philippians 3:20-21), our new bodies will be free from gravity. As an example, our Lord was able to ascend from earth to heaven at will as described in Acts 1. We can reason from the differences between this present body and our new body that the new heaven and the new earth will be different in essence from what we now know. Our current body is designed for service in our current environment. We breathe oxygen, which is produced by plants. We can tolerate free nitrogen. The temperatures we experience are compatible with life. The sun is the ideal distance from earth. We have both plant and animal food. Since our coming spiritual body will be fundamentally different, we can reason that our future environment will likewise be very different. Indeed Revelation 21 & 22 tell us so.

Just as our body will be free from present limitations, so will our mind. Consider 1 Corinthians 13:12: *"For now we see through a glass darkly, but then face to face. Now I know in part, but then I shall know even as I am fully known."* This is saying that in the resurrection I shall have the same knowledge as does Jesus Christ. Instead of misusing this knowledge, I shall be in perfect harmony with Him and in perfect subjection to Him. I will then know everything that He knows, astounding as this seems. Yet I will remain subject to Him with perfect contentment. I will also be in perfect delight to be in that blessed state. All questions of rank and authority that cause so many troubles on earth will be gone. We will all be in the immediate presence of God and in perfect subjection to Him.

The Scriptures do give us some specific details about the resurrection body of our Lord Jesus, most specifically in Luke 24. He was able to appear to be an ordinary human being to the two disciples on the Emmaus road. He spoke and reasoned with them from the Scriptures. When He entered the Upper Room, the risen Christ had no need to open a door. Instead He passed right through the walls. He was able to eat, although He had no need to eat. When He instituted the Lord's Supper, He promised that He would drink it new in His Father's Kingdom after His resurrection (Matthew 26:29). His resurrection body is capable of appearing human, but it may also shine brilliantly as in the Transfiguration (Matthew 17:1-9) and even beyond that intensity as in Revelation 1. Our body will be like His, although we will never have or desire His authority.

When we consider the implications of our bodies and minds being like that of our Lord Jesus, we can start with His ability to hear all prayer in all languages at one time. In one fashion or another we will have perfect communication in heaven, with the consequences of the Tower of Babel being undone. He can be present anywhere and everywhere at once. Like a multi-tasking computer but on a much higher plane, we will be able to serve our Lord in several ways at once. To frame an example that lacks imagination, we might sing praises, tend gardens and lay our crown before Him all at one time even in separate locations. Or perhaps location as a concept will have no meaning in heaven. Earthly light and darkness make no difference to Him now (Psalm 139:11-12). We will not even have darkness in heaven (Revelation 22:5). There will be no sleep and yet no pain nor fatigue.

With the absence of the Sun, God Himself will be the light of the New Jerusalem (Revelation 22:5). I cannot say how our new eyes might be adapted to this change, but it will happen. Our hearing will likewise be suited to the new heavenly music. There is much more that we cannot know now but that we will learn in due time.

In 1 Corinthians 13:13, we are told that for now we must have faith, hope and love. In the new heaven and the new earth with our new bodies and minds faith and hope will be fulfilled totally. That leaves love as the greatest of the three because love will remain in the new heavens and new earth to come. If the Lake of Fire is unadulterated fury, then heaven is pure love, as represented by the marriage supper there.

JUDGMENT FOR THE BELIEVER: REWARDS AND LOSSES

Once one realizes that human existence is everlasting beyond the grave and beyond the Last Judgment, it is sensible to focus first on the infinite differences between Heaven and the Lake of Fire. But the Scriptures also teach that there are everlasting rewards for faithful service among believers headed for heaven. Scriptures also warn that rewards in heaven, although not salvation, can be forfeited. Some argue that it is legalistic to strive for these rewards, pointing out that we will reach Heaven by grace and grace alone. That is true. But entry into any rewards that God offers is equally by grace, not by unaided human power. The ideas of grace and of rewards seem inconsistent, but we must remember that grace is offered initially to the spiritually dead while rewards are offered only to those who are already spiritually alive. There is no inconsistency with God. His offer of rewards recognizes the fundamental difference between our initial state of spiritual death (Ephesians 2:1-10) and our altered state of spiritual life after salvation by grace through faith. For the living believer, God well knows and uses the power of incentive. My statement may seem logical, but neither you nor I should accept this without support from Scripture.

According to the grace of God which is given unto me, as a wise master builder, I have laid the foundation, and another builds on it. But let every man take heed how he builds on it.

For another foundation can no man lay than that is laid, which is Jesus Christ.

Now if any man build upon this foundation gold, silver, precious stones, wood, hay, stubble;

Every man's work shall be made manifest: for the Day shall declare it, because it shall be revealed by fire; and the fire shall try every man's work of what sort it is.

If any man's work abide which he has built thereupon, he shall receive a reward.

If any man's work shall be burned, he shall suffer loss: but he himself shall be saved out of the fire. 1 Corinthians 3:10-15 (the last words of verse 15 altered from the KJV based in the Interlinear Greek New Testament of the Textus Receptus of George Ricker Berry)

Consider Nehemiah's repeated prayers:

Think upon me, my God, for good, [according] to all that I have done for this people. Nehemiah 5:19

Remember me, O my God, concerning this, and wipe not out my good deeds that I have done for the house of my God, and for the offices of it. Nehemiah 13:14

Remember me, O my God, [concerning] this also, and spare me according to the greatness of Your mercy. Nehemiah 13:22

Remember me, O my God, for good. Nehemiah 13:31

Consider the words of the Lord Jesus Himself:

Rejoice, and be exceeding glad: for great is your reward in heaven: for so persecuted they the prophets which were before you. Matthew 5:12 in the context of persecution for the faith; see also Luke 6:23

He that receives a prophet in the name of a prophet shall receive a prophet's reward; and he that receives a righteous man in the name of a righteous man shall receive a righteous man's reward. Matthew 10:41

And whosoever shall give to drink unto one of these little ones a cup of cold [water] only in the name of a disciple, verily I say unto you, he shall in no wise lose his reward. Matthew 10:42, also Mark 9:41

But love your enemies, and do good, and lend, hoping for nothing again; and your reward shall be great, and you shall be the children of the Highest: for He is kind to the unthankful and the evil. Luke 6:35

Then one also has these quotes from various epistles:

Now he that plants and he that waters are one: and every man shall receive his own reward according to his own labor. 1 Corinthians 3:8

Let no man beguile you of your reward in a voluntary humility and worshiping of angels, intruding into those things which he has not seen, vainly puffed up by his fleshly mind . . . Colossians 2:18

Knowing that of the Lord you shall receive the reward of the inheritance: for you serve the Lord Christ. Colossians 3:24

Cast not away therefore your confidence, which hath great compensation of reward. Hebrews 10:35

Esteeming the reproach of Christ greater riches than the treasures in Egypt: for he had respect unto the compensation of the reward. Hebrews 11:26 (speaking of Moses)

Look to yourselves, that we lose not those things which we have worked, but that we receive a full reward. 2 John 8

And the nations were angry, and Your wrath is come, and the time of the dead, that they should be judged, and that You should give reward unto Your servants the prophets, and to the saints, and them that fear Your name, small and great; and should destroy them which destroy the earth. Revelation 11:18

And, behold, I come quickly; and My reward is with Me, to give every man according as his work shall be. Revelation 22:12 spoken by the resurrected Lord Jesus

The Apostle Paul referred to the ancient Olympic Games in 1 Corinthians 9:24-27. In that time there were laurels only for the winners, unlike the modern practice of gold, silver and bronze medals. Paul through the Holy Spirit exhorted his readers, *"So run that you may obtain."* As the Olympic laurels were strong incentives to the ancient athlete, so the rewards of Christ must be to us.

We should conclude that there is ample teaching in Holy Scripture for the idea that Jesus Christ will reward His saved people according to their good works. *"And their works do follow them."* Revelation 14:13. Consider also the parable of the talents. The believer who managed and invested 10 minas was then given 10 cities. The next believer who managed and invested 5 minas was then given 5 cities. Luke 19:12-27. Rewards are proportioned to faithfulness and effectiveness.

The rewards are especially great when we must suffer for the sake of Jesus Christ. Peter said that it is better to suffer for right than for wrong. 1 Peter 3:14-17. Our Lord Jesus went further, promising great reward as compensation for suffering for His sake, teaching in Matthew 19:29 that *"everyone that has forsaken houses, or brethren, or sisters, or father, or mother, or wife, or children, or lands, for My name's sake, shall receive an hundredfold, and shall inherit everlasting life."*

Still another confirmation that we can and should look forward to heavenly rewards comes from the seven letters that the Lord Jesus sent to the seven churches in Revelation 2 & 3. The Ephesian church in Revelation 2:7 was promised, *"To him that overcomes will I give to eat of the tree of life, which is in the midst of the paradise of God."* What a wonderful promise! The very thing that Adam and Eve were forbidden to do is now given as a reward. That means the reversal of death and eternal life. So the most basic consequence of Satan's temptation of Adam and Eve (and by extension of us also) is reversed!

The church at Smyrna in Revelation 2:10 was given this promise: *"Fear none of those things which you shalt suffer: behold, the devil shall cast some of you into prison, that you may be tried; and you shall have tribulation ten days: you be faithful unto death, and I will give you a crown of life."* As a complement to the promise to the Ephesians, we are given the promise of a crown of life, as we are a *"a royal priesthood, a holy nation . . ."* 1 Peter 2:9.

Even though the church at Pergamos had significant issues within it, the promises are great. Our risen Lord Jesus said, *"To him that overcomes will I give to eat of the hidden manna, and will give him a white stone, and in the stone a new name written, which no man knows saving he that receives."* Revelation 2:17. I am informed by those knowledgeable in Greek culture that a "white stone" symbolized acquittal as comes with a verdict of "not guilty." Like a person in a witness protection program, although not for the same reasons, we also receive a new name and a whole new identity as holy and without sin. There is precedent: Abram became Abraham, Sarai became Sarah, Jacob became Israel and Saul of Tarsus became Paul the Apostle. God indeed will make all things new, including us.

To the faithful within the church of Thyatira the Lord Jesus gave a promise in Revelation 2:26-27 that also connects with our royalty in 1 Peter 2:9: *"And he that overcomes, and keeps My works unto the end, to him will I give power over the nations: And he shall rule them with a rod of iron; as the vessels of a potter shall they be broken to shivers: even as I received of my Father."* We will be allowed to sit with our Lord Jesus in His throne (Revelation 3:21), just as a child may sit with his or her parent in the office. And then in addition, *"And I will give him the Morning Star."* Revelation 2:28.

Sardis was a church in trouble, like a bush with life in only a small proportion of branches with mostly dead branches (think of John 15:1-6 for the terrible implications of spiritual deadness). Our Lord Jesus had a promise for them that indicates both acquittal and purity, recorded in Revelation 3:4-5: *"You have a few names even in Sardis which have not defiled their garments; and they shall walk with Me in white: for they are worthy. He that overcomes, the same shall be clothed in white clothing; and I will not blot out his name out of the Book of Life, but I will confess his name before My Father, and before His angels."* We should not skip over the promise that our name will not be blotted out of the Book of Life. This means everlasting salvation and means that we will be found in the Book of Life at the judgment described in the last part of Revelation 20.

The church in Philadelphia was given a precious promise relating to the enemies of the church which is a blessing to all true Christians and churches who face enemies: *"Behold, I will make them of the synagogue of Satan, which say they are Jews, and are not, but do lie; behold, I will make them to come and worship before your feet, and to know that I have loved you."* Revelation 3:9. In the first century before the Jewish revolt in Jerusalem starting in 66 AD, Jews and Gentiles either separately or in combination sometimes attacked Christians. They combined to crucify Jesus Christ, with the High Priest and his allies having a leading part in that injustice and Pontius Pilate a secondary part. The Apostle Paul was chased by Jews from Thessalonica as far as Berea but also by idolatrous Gentile silversmiths in Ephesus. In Philadelphia apparently the church had Jewish enemies who are pointed out here. But Nero, the dissolute Roman Emperor, separately became a vicious enemy of Christians throughout the Empire and became a special target of God's anger in Revelation 13. What I am seeking to avoid is provoking prejudice against either Jews or Gentiles by pointing out that at times both unbelieving Jews and unbelieving Gentiles have rebelled against God to the point of persecuting Christians because they are Christians. All nationalities have their full share of sin, including our own.

The blessing of Jesus Christ to the church in Philadelphia continues in Revelation 3:10-12:

Because you have kept the word of my patience, I also will keep you from the hour of temptation, which shall come upon all the world, to try them that dwell upon the earth.

Behold, I come quickly: hold that fast which you have, that no man take thy crown.

Him that overcomes will I make a pillar in the temple of my God, and he shall go no more out: and I will write upon him the name of my God, and the name of the city of my God, new Jerusalem, which comes down out of heaven from my God: and [I will write upon him] my new name.

First we should note that we are exhorted in verse 11 to hang on to our crowns in the midst of an evil world where many will try to take our crowns away. In verse 12 we are promised stability and an everlasting place in the presence of God, and that God will label us with His name. This complements the promise of a new name for ourselves given to the church in Pergamos.

Verse 10 is saved for last because it is more controversial. We can be sure that it involves the Rapture of the Church to save it from the judgment of God which will crash down on the entire earth. If you refer to the cycles in Revelation, you will note the first instance of worldwide judgment at the end of Revelation 6. The others can be located in the last portion of Revelation 14 and in Revelation 16. Yet in individual cases God often took His saints out of the earth through physical death to spare them misery. King Josiah's death at age 39 just before the first Babylonian invasion is one such instance. See 2 Kings 23:26-30; 2 Chronicles 35:20-27. And Isaiah says, *"The righteous perishes, and no man lays it to heart: and merciful men are taken away, none considering that the righteous is taken away from the evil to come."* Isaiah 57:1. In addition to the Rapture at the very last of the Christian Church, I would not exclude instances in which God has taken Christians home to heaven instead of leaving them to face miseries on earth from the reach of the promise of Revelation 3:10. There is a time to die as well as to live if we do not reach the Rapture in this mortal body. The point is to lay up treasure in heaven (Matthew 6:19-21) and to seek reward there whether our physical life span should prove to be short, medium or long, and whether it should reach the Rapture or not.

THE THESSALONIAN WITNESS

One essential truth as to the order of events in the Last Days is found in 2 Thessalonians 2:2-5. From the text, it appears that some teachers were claiming that the Day of the Lord was either just around the corner or (in some translations) already past. Looking at the literal Greek, the most natural reading of the proposition that Paul was correcting is that the Day of the Lord is almost here and could come at any moment. Paul states that the Anti-Christ must first be revealed before the Messiah will return. An event closely linked with the revealing of the Anti-Christ ("the man of sin, the son of perdition"—2 Thessalonians 2:3) is an apostasy ("falling away" in verse 3, Greek apostasia, probably corresponding to Christ's warning in Matthew 24:12 that in the end times the love of many [or of the many, i.e. the majority] will grow cold). When the Anti-Christ is revealed, (meaning that his character will be concealed for a time, which would fit the idea in one layer of Daniel 9:24-27 that the Anti-Christ will make and then break a covenant with Israel. Israel would not make the covenant if it recognized the Anti-Christ for who he is.) he will also appear in the Temple claiming to be God and demanding worship. Leaving aside for the moment the question of what will constitute the Temple in that context, it is clear that the Anti-Christ is literally trying to supplant Jesus Christ as the ruler of Israel and of all humanity. I think that his next intended step in league with Satan would be to attack God Himself, as may have been intended with the Tower of Babel. The Greek myths contain an echo of speculation in that the Greek gods supposedly overthrew their parents. But such nonsense and rebellion will never get that far, although that observation jumps ahead in sequence. For the moment, the major point is that the revelation of the Anti-Christ and the apostasy that comes with it must precede the return of the Lord. History seems to be building rapidly toward that apostasy now, although we cannot give any timetable.

Paul makes a similar point in 2 Timothy 2:18 in condemning teachers who taught that the resurrection is past already. We do know from 1 Corinthians 15:23-24 that the resurrection is associated closely and essentially simultaneous with the return of Jesus Christ. *"Christ the firstfruits, then they that are Christ's at His coming. Then comes the end . . ."* Since the resurrection is yet future, the return of the Lord is likewise future. Both follow the apostasy triggered by persecution of which the Lord Jesus warned in Matthew 24.

If the apostasy comes first, why is most of the world blindsided by the coming of our Lord until it is too late? One reason is the spiritual delusion mentioned in 2 Thessalonians 2:11, but 1 Thessalonians 5:3 gives a clue. The world will be expecting and longing for "peace and safety." This will be a massive case of wishful thinking. If my dual understanding of Daniel 9:24-27 is correct, then the expectation of "peace and safety" will probably stem from the false covenant of the Anti-Christ, which will paper over the issues of the Middle East and give the illusion of peace. On another level, Revelation 11 in its beginning shows a precarious restraint of the power of the Anti-Christ by the power of the two witnesses in Jerusalem to impose miracles of judgment (suggestive of the plagues that doomed Pharaoh in Exodus). When those two witnesses are killed (the timing of 3½ years suggests they are killed as part of the violation of the false covenant), the Anti-Christ is not subject to further restraint on earth (note the removal of the divine restraint prophesied in 2 Thessalonians 2:7-8). People celebrate their deaths on earth as if it is Christmas or Hanukkah. Following the resurrection of the two witnesses, the Anti-Christ turns on Israel and on Christians wherever he can locate them, as shown in Revelation 13. The 42 months of Revelation 13:5 matches the time period of Revelation 11:2. I think that they coincide with one another as the last and worst half of the worldwide replay of the 70th week which originally was fulfilled in miniature by the destruction of Israel and the Temple by the Romans ending in 70 AD. One portrays the oppression of Jerusalem and the attack that climaxes at Armageddon; the other portrays the final persecution of Christianity and the filling up of the martyrs. The bodily return of the Lord Jesus brings both of these trends to a screeching halt. So the world is blindsided for the false joy that it experiences when it thinks that it has succeeded in escaping the restraint of God.

Psalm 2 gives an overview of this, finishing with the destruction of the wicked and an exhortation to submit to God now while there is yet time to do so. That last hateful generation will be blindsided, but that is no reason for you to be blind when Jesus as the Light of the World illuminates the truth for you.

Another point as to sequence is made in 1 Thessalonians 4:13-18, dealing with the sequence between the resurrection of the deceased saints and the rapture of the living saints at the return of our Lord. Verses 15-17 state beyond doubt that the dead in Christ rise before the living saints are raptured. No order of events of the Last Days can be correct if it places the rapture of the Church before the resurrection of those who have died in Christ before His return, with one possible exception to be discussed in the next paragraph. The pre-tribulation explanations of the Rapture that I have heard violate this principle.

In the previous paragraph I left Revelation 20 aside for the sake of clarity. It introduces a new element that I do not believe had been mentioned in previous prophecy. Read without symbolism, Revelation 20:4 introduces the martyrs for the Lord Jesus, and verse 5 indicates that they are raised from the dead 1000 years earlier than the rest of the dead, who would be conscious but lack a resurrection body. Revelation is rich in symbolism, but no symbolism is apparent here. The text appears to say that the martyrs as an extra reward for their faithfulness to death receive 1000 years with Jesus Christ on earth (along with the survivors of the Tribulation and their descendants). While this line of thought does not require multiple judgments, it does posit multiple resurrections. There is authority for this; Matthew 27:52-53 says that many Old Testament saints arose when the Lord Jesus arose from the dead and appeared to people in Jerusalem (on their way from the grave to heaven). There is no consensus within the Church on the question of the Millenium on earth, but Revelation 20 seems to teach one. So we get an order of events:

The Tribulation of 7 years begins, probably with the false covenant;

Halfway through the Tribulation, the false covenant is broken and the two faithful witnesses of Revelation 11 are martyred;

The second half of the Tribulation brings intensified persecution (Revelation 13 and Matthew 24 running concurrently) and unparalleled judgments, including natural disasters literally of Biblical proportions;

The return of Jesus Christ to earth cuts short the Tribulation when it is about to cause the extermination of the human race (Matthew 24:22), and also brings with it the resurrection of the martyred dead in Christ. The Beast and the False Prophet are thrown alive into the Lake of Fire and Satan is made a prisoner in the bottomless pit of Revelation 20. This starts the 1000 years of Christ's personal reign on earth and fulfills many prophecies of earthly blessing, particularly in Isaiah. In heavenly time, this is the equivalent of one day (2 Peter 3:8). I do not profess to understand how this stretching of time will work or feel, but I think that Einstein did theorize that such warping of time would be possible; and

At the close of the Millenium, Satan is released and stirs up a new rebellion of most of the human race. This is stopped by God using fire from heaven. Then the rest of the dead are raised and judged. Satan and the wicked are cast into the Lake of Fire. The righteous are united with the martyrs already raised from the dead with new bodies, and Jesus Christ reigns in joy over one combined flock of believers from both Israel by physical descent and from all nations.

Paul in 2 Thessalonians 1:9 summarizes the punishment of the unbelieving majority (Matthew 7:13-14), *"who shall be punished with everlasting destruction from the presence of the Lord and from the glory of His power."* The previous verse mentions "flaming fire." I do not know the precise mechanism of this aspect of the punishment, but I can offer some analogies to things experienced on earth. Many of us have seen newsreels of people shrouded in napalm, which often sticks to the person. Others may be familiar with white phosphorus, which keeps burning. Both give us some idea of the persistence of this punishment, which last forever without respite. Both of these weapons cause horrible injuries in war, but neither one matches up to the ultimate punishment in the Lake of Fire.

The destruction of the wicked is not confined to fire as we know it. Oxidation gives off light, which is absent in the Lake of Fire. It will be so dark that one cannot see a hand in front of one's nose. Jude 6, 13. If one has functioning eyes in the Lake of Fire, it would make no difference because there will be only blackness, probably more intense than the darkness in Egypt in Moses' time. Exodus 10:21-23. The darkness superimposes a punishment of the mind—of sensory deprivation—on top of the physical pain. With the brimstone, the inhabitants of the Lake of Fire will be inhaling sulfurous gases, which would probably cause nausea or constant gagging or both.

Then we know that the inhabitants of the Lake of Fire will be subject to divine derision from Psalm 2:6. I do not know what message God might send, but I know that the inhabitants will hate it. The rebels will be belittled forever. Imagine the scorn of modern media a million times over, running forever. In old professional wrestling shows, there was a character named Jimmy Hart ("the mouth of the South", although his accent sounded like New York) who could be most annoying with a megaphone. An alternative might be the constant self-confession forced upon a prisoner in a Communist re-education camp. But those ended, whereas this will never end or even take a break. They were part of an act or often based in falsehood, but in the Lake of Fire all the accusations will be true. There will be no way to shake them off. At the very least, the punishment of the wicked has concurrent elements of excruciating physical pain both from external burning and internal organs (Revelation 14:10, 16:19), of perpetual darkness and of non-stop condemnation. God's mercy will be totally absent. For this reason the righteous need not concern themselves about any unfairness in their treatment by other people. God will take care of that.

The most important principle concerning the Rapture does not deal with sequence at all. The last portion of 1 Thessalonians 4:17-18 reads: *"So shall we ever be with the Lord. Wherefore, comfort one another with these words."* Through the Spirit Paul exults: *"Then shall be brought to pass the saying that is written, 'Death is swallowed up in victory.' O death, where is your sting? O grave, where is your victory? The sting of death is sin and the strength of sin is the law. But thanks be to God Who gives us the victory through the Lord Jesus Christ."* 1 Corinthians 15:54-57. On this basis we are commanded to be steadfast. Whether we are raptured or pass through physical death it remains true that *"For me to live is Christ and to die is gain."* Philippians 1:21. 2 Corinthians 5 also deals with this truth. And note what Revelation 14:12 says in the immediate context of the judgment of the wicked: *"Here is the patience of the saints. Here are they who keep the commandments of God and the faith of Jesus."* As a general observation, most Christians shy away from the subject of the judgment of the wicked and the deliverance that Jesus Christ will give to His own at His return to earth. The ostracism that we face now will be gone. The injustices will be undone. Whereas the wicked face God's eternal hatred, we will receive His eternal love. The wicked will suffer forever in their sinful state (Revelation 22:11) and our partial, tentative holiness will become complete holiness and complete intimacy with the Father, Son and Holy Spirit. We need to keep these truths fresh in our minds to give us grace to endure the trials and tribulations that we must face before heaven. (Acts 14:22, Romans 5:3)

Your reaction to this may be that God is cruel beyond reason. From the viewpoint of raw power, it does make sense to surrender to Jesus Christ just as it made sense for a king with a smaller army to negotiate to avoid battle. Luke 14:31-32. Beyond that, heaven cannot be heaven without justice being done. We rarely reflect on how serious it is to contradict God. Our unbelief and our defiance of God is an insult to the very Father Who has given us life and so many things that make life bearable. The offense is eternal because we have offended an eternal God. If on top of that we reject the sacrifice of His eternal Son as our substitute, what else is left but eternal punishment? Having been made in the image of God, we cannot cease from existing. The only question is whether we will exist in love and fellowship with God in heaven or as a perpetual captive in hatred and rebellion against God in the Lake of Fire?

As a lawyer, let me take you through an analogous situation that I have handled countless times as a defense counsel. If you were caught red-handed on multiple counts of selling illegal drugs, it would avail nothing with a judge to protest that our drug laws makes no sense to you and for that reason you should be let off. A defendant must accept the law as it is and cannot remake it according to his or her own standards. Even more so this is true of divine justice, where God Himself is the author of the law to judge your conduct, words and thoughts. In human justice, many times I have been able to negotiate a reduction in the severity of the charges as a measure of damage control or as consideration for my client's cooperation against worse offenders. In divine justice, Jesus Christ has no need of human cooperation because He already knows everything. So anyone is up against it with a choice of admitting guilt or of trying to maintain innocence against overwhelming evidence. Unlike human justice, there is no bargaining with God—you either accept His terms of total surrender to the mercy of His Son or you can vainly try to maintain your innocence despite the evidence. In human justice, most people negotiate rather than maintain innocence to the last, although I have seen a murderer refuse to negotiate. But when it comes to divine justice, people so hate Jesus Christ that they refuse His mercy because it involves personal surrender to the Lordship of Jesus Christ. And so they end up being perpetually broken by His justice. You violate God's Law but you cannot break it. It breaks you. My appeal for repentance does have in its background the love and mercy of God through His Son the Lord Jesus, but at first you may know little or nothing about that love and mercy. For many people that knowledge comes after salvation. So I am approaching you based on something within your own experience. People have enough sense to surrender when facing overwhelming power. If you are not a disciple of Jesus Christ, you are precisely in that place. Surrender now and trust that His love will come to you later. It will.

Much as it may be against your natural inclination, I urge you as one of many ambassadors of Jesus Christ (2 Corinthians 5:20) to bow your heart and spirit and worship Him as the Son of God. Let Him own you as Lord and Savior; He has already paid the sacrifice necessary to free human beings from sin. Ask Him to set you free from your sin and from Satan so that you can serve Him instead. You will be amazed at the joy that God will bring with salvation, even if trouble comes with the joy. In losing your self-will, you will receive eternal life which is infinitely better.

REVELATION CYCLES
OF JUDGMENT

There are at least three cycles in Revelation, each in a series of seven. Seven is a number of completion. In sports a championship series is best of seven. We have seven days in a week. Noah took seven pairs of every clean animal into the Ark. In Revelation there is a phrase which has been translated either as "the seven Spirits of God" or as the "seven-fold Spirit of God." In either case the number seven denotes a complete sequence.

The first of these cycles starts in Revelation 6 with the seven seals. In the order written, the seals are:

A) The man on the white horse—the conqueror;
B) General worldwide warfare;
C) Food shortage to the point of famine;
D) Death of 25% of the world population;
E) Martyrdom and the prayers of the martyrs for justice;
F) Earthquake shakes the earth and the heavens are also shaken (Haggai 2:6-7); and
G) In chapter 7 a vision of the salvation of Israel in contrast to the judgments just shown.

We need not assume that chapter 7 is necessarily chronologically immediately behind chapter 6. It is possible to view chapter 7 as an introduction to the earthly Millenium, which would make it chronological. That is my inclination. This goes back to the interpretation of Revelation 20. It is also possible to view chapter 7, showing salvation, as showing contrast with chapter 6 showing disaster rather than strict time sequence. Unlike a movie, a book must portray only one picture at a time even when the actions are simultaneous or overlapping.

The second cycle of seven trumpets starts in Revelation 8. In this series the judgments are:

A) Hail and fire, burning 1/3rd of the vegetation;

B) A fiery mountain is cast into the sea, causing 1/3rd of the sea to turn to blood, probably like the Nile River during the plagues of Moses before the Exodus;

C) One-third of the drinking water becomes bitter and undrinkable;

D) One-third of the sun and stars are blotted out, reducing light to the earth;

So far the judgments are partial, which leads me to the inference that these four trumpets correspond to the first half of the 7-year tribulation period rather than to the second half. There is still an implied opening for repentance in that God is yet showing some restraint in the extent of the judgments.

E) Locusts that torment like scorpions, causing pain so severe that human beings will desire to die but will be unable to do so. Rather they must endure the torment, a foreshadowing of the torments of the Lake of Fire to come after. These locusts may also have a symbolic significance of demon activity.

F) The release of demons from the Euphrates River in order to open the way for an army from the Orient, to usher in mass warfare not precedented even by World War 2. This looks like the prelude to Armageddon and together with other simultaneous judgments results in the death of one-third of the human race, and

G) The seventh trumpet again shifts the scene to heaven as did the seventh seal, where John is given another prophecy. However, the seventh seal is said to finish the mystery of God.

The third cycle of seven bowls or vials start in Revelation 16.

A) Vile sores upon the worshippers of the Anti-Christ;
B) 100% of the sea becomes blood—all sea life wiped out (like the 2nd trumpet except for total destruction instead of 1/3rd destruction)
C) 100% of fresh surface water becomes blood, like the 3rd trumpet except for total destruction instead of 1/3rd destruction
D) Sun strengthened, humans scorched (compared to 4th trumpet where the sun and stars are 1/3rd blotted out, going from probable freezing cold to oven-like heat)
E) Darkness, probably like the darkness of Egypt during its plagues
F) Euphrates River dries up, opening the way for the Oriental army (similar to the 6th trumpet)
G) Monstrous earthquake corresponding to the 6th seal and fiery hail, probably like the hail of the plague preceding the Exodus.

Chapters 17 and 18 give a different perspective on these events, stressing the spiritual judgments upon unbelief and false religion. Chapter 19 views the preparation for the marriage supper of the Lamb of God with His people, which preparation probably proceeds parallel with the judgments upon the earth. In terms of time, the events of chapter 7 and 19 probably overlap and may even be completely simultaneous. The 6th seal of Revelation 6 and the 7th vial of Revelation 16 are the same event, so Revelation should be visualized like the movie that John saw in three cycles of 7 rather than a linear book written in strict chronological order. Also note that the original 1/3rd environmental destruction of the trumpets is later completed as total destruction of the same environment in later vials. In between, the sad but true verdict against humanity as a whole is recorded in Revelation 9:20-21: *"And the rest of the men that were not killed by these plagues yet did not repent of the works of their hands, that they should not worship demons and idols of gold, silver and brass and of stone, silver and wood, which neither can see, nor hear, nor walk; neither did they repent of their murders, nor of their [drug-connected—Greek word pharmakos] sorceries, nor of their fornication nor of their thefts.* [For the preparation of this table I should give thanks to Pastor John Malcolm of Port Charlotte, Florida for his insight that each cycle closes with a scene in heaven. He and I independently came to the same basic views on the cycles of Revelation. One corollary is that we both believe that Revelation 7 and 14 are two different views of the same scene.]

	SEALS	*TRUMPETS*	*BOWLS/VIALS*
First	*6:1-2*	*Rev. 8:7*	*Rev. 16:2*
	Conqueror	*Fiery hail—partial destruction of greenery 1/3rd of trees; all grass*	*Foul sores on the skin of those who worship the Anti-Christ*
Second	*6:3-4*	*Rev. 8:8-9*	*Rev. 16:3*
	Massive war	*One-third of sea becomes blood; one-third of marine life killed*	*Sea became as blood; all life in the sea dies*
Third	*6:5-6*	*Rev. 8:10-11*	*Rev. 16:4-7*
	Partial famine	*Wormwood—one-third of fresh water becomes bitter and unusable*	*Fresh water becomes blood*
Fourth	*6:7-8*	*Rev. 8:12-13*	*Rev. 16:8-9*

	25% death	*One-third of sun and moon struck—partial darkness for 1/3 of day and night*	*Sun strengthened causing scorching heat; People refuse to repent (see also 9:20-21)*
Fifth	*6:9-11*	*9:1-11*	*Rev. 16:10-11*
	Prayers of the martyrs for vengeance to be shortly granted in full	*Scorpion-like locusts released to torment but not kill unbelievers. The scorpions may be symbolic or real, but the pain is clearly real.*	*Darkness in kingdom of the Anti-Christ like the plague of Exodus. Again people blaspheme God and refuse to repent.*
Sixth	*6:12-17*	*9:13-19*	*Rev. 16:12-14*
	Massive earthquake (compare 8:5 also); disturbances in the sky and outer space and rejected prayers of humanity to be hidden from Almighty God	*Evil spirits released from Euphrates—river dries up for the kings of the east, leading to massive warfare and one-third death*	*Evil spirits released from Euphrates; they gather the world to Armageddon for battle*
Seventh	*Rev. 8:1*	*Rev. 11:15-19*	*Rev. 16:16-21*
	Silence in heaven for 30 minutes (see also the stillness of 7:1)	*Jesus Christ takes over all the kingdoms of this world—also earthquake and great hail*	*Massive earthquake and great hail on earth*

REVELATION 9:21 AS A SUMMARY OF GOD'S JUDGMENT UPON THE WORLD SYSTEM (Greek *kosmos*)

Revelation 9:21 lists four sins that humanity will cling to with stubbornness in the face of the judgments of God: (1) Murders; (2) Drug-induced sorceries; (3) Fornications; and (4) Thefts. The previous verse denounces with worship of man-made false gods in preference to the true God, which underlies the sins of Revelation 9:21. In this respect God in His anger allows humanity a taste of what it wants. Upon reflection one realizes that the four listed sins undermine the cornerstones of civilization. God permits this because He is about to sweep aside all human government in favor of direct dictatorial rule by Jesus Christ, His Son. Ordinarily, we should shrink with horror from dictatorship, but Jesus Christ is the one exception because He is perfect and can bear absolute power without sin and without error.

The first function of any human government is the preservation of human life. When human government was instituted, Noah was given the command of capital punishment for murder. Genesis 9:5-6. Even dictatorship is preferable to anarchy, where nobody is safe when asleep and can be safe only by superior force when awake. In such anarchy the lack of security will prevent peaceful pursuits such as agriculture and will kill from lack of sleep or lack of food. When the Roman Empire fell in Western Europe, a system of feudalism arose that had the minimum virtue of enough protection to permit subsistence crops to be grown. But that system had virtually no freedom. Innovation was glacial. Literacy was rare. Where less energy could be applied to protecting human life, more could be applied to learning and innovation. But now civilizations around the world are violating en masse the essential principle of the sanctity of human life that God laid down in the beginning with Cain and then with Noah. Against the lessons of history and above all against the words of Holy Scripture, human life is considered to be disposable once again. This is the prelude to the massive loss of human life that will arise during the Tribulation.

In Asia, abortions are often directed at girls in order to avoid the cost of dowries. This will mean a surplus of men over women, which generally is a prelude to war and lawlessness. Male-female birth ratios are already skewed in substantial parts of Asia. Indeed war and lawlessness are predicted as characteristic of the Last Days and Revelation does predict a massive army from the east (Revelation 9:16, 16:12) as converging on Armageddon. We cannot say how quickly this is coming nor with certainty that the present sex-selective abortion pattern in parts of Asia is part of the build-up to the main event, but that very possibility should be a warning to *"lay not up treasures on earth where moth and rust corrupt and where thieves break through and steal, but to lay up treasures in heaven where moth and rust do not corrupt nor do thieves break through and steal. For where your treasure is your heart will be also."* Matthew 6:19-21.

The second corner of civilization that is collapsing is reasoning. This is being undermined by the use of mind-bending drugs from marijuana to cocaine to methamphetamine to hallucinogens to bath salts. New mind-destroying drugs are still being found and marketed and alcohol is used in sufficient quantities to destroy the minds of many. God said to falling Israel, *"Come, let us reason together, says the Lord. Though your sins be as scarlet, they shall be as white as snow. Thought they be red like crimson, they shall be as wool."* Isaiah 1:18. The Lord Jesus used reason in offering analogies to the people. Two examples of many are found in Luke 14:31 and in Matthew 22:31-32. But humanity as a whole is disposed to destroy its own ability to reason by the use of mind-destroying drugs. In so doing humanity is also cutting communications with God. Humanity as a whole does not want to hear what He has to say.

The third corner of civilization that is collapsing is the family. An essential of family life is sexual faithfulness between one husband and one wife. From a theological perspective, I have written in some detail in my previous book Assault on Marriage: A Christian Response. Viewing the aspect of the family's contribution to civilization, we are relearning the lesson of how important an intact marriage is for the growth of healthy children to form the basis of the following generation. Any police detective or true crime writer can remind us that most individual murders outside of abortion involve shattered marriages, frequently because of sexual infidelity. Another share involves perverted sex of many types, including crimes against children. The vast increase in crimes within the family is a terrible toxin from the breakdown of sexual faithfulness. Another consequence is the moral fragility and lack of initiative on the part of most older children. Young people depend on others instead of learning to stand on their own feet. This is important both in economic and spiritual life; a Christian must stand against the current because genuinely converted Christians are most often in the minority. God gave us the Eighth Commandment for our good, but humanity as a whole rejects it and fouls its own nest.

The fourth corner of civilization that is collapsing is private property. This is the foundation of incentives and economic life. We have seen societies in which private property is virtually absent, such as Stalinist Russia, Cambodia under the Khmer Rouge and Maoist China. All were disasters from which even Communist ideologues have been forced to recoil. But France is trying to raise marginal tax rates to 75%. Phil Mickelson recently complained with justice that he will be paying a total marginal tax rate near 63%. When government makes such outsized claims, private property suffers as does the incentive to go on working. Private property is an important means for families to form and to stick together. It likewise is a vital buffer so that a person or family can live without being dependent on government. Private property functions as a check on the ambitions of government officials for more and more power. God protects private property by the Seventh Commandment. Samuel, the prophet-priest, warned of excessive taxation in 1 Samuel 8. Private property is being eroded in much of the civilized world both by excessive government and by private theft, especially fraud. Could the deterioration in the health of private property in the Western world be a prelude to the Last Days? We do not know but we cannot rule it out.

Before we go further in examining the sequence of the events of the last seven years before the Second Coming, we should take an overview to view the overall results of the rule of the Anti-Christ, which God permits for a short time as a tool of judgment before the Anti-Christ is himself judged. To put this another way, God will one day deliver the world to the authority of the Anti-Christ as punishment for the sins of the world for which there is no repentance and therefore no atonement. In turn, God will punish the Anti-Christ even though the Anti-Christ will have unwittingly fulfilled the decree of God, most especially because the Anti-Christ will have sought worship as God and have committed grossly sinful and brutal acts for his own motives. Each is guilty of his own sinful thoughts, actions and omissions even though that sin is a part of God's sovereign design. (Romans 9:18-23) As James points out, God is never the author of sin (James 1:13 compare Acts 2:23), but God is sovereign over all things and all people, including wicked rulers (for example Proverbs 21:1, compare 1 Corinthians 2:1-8). So even the Anti-Christ is unwillingly under the restraint of God in everything he may do, even when he thinks he is turned loose to do his worst. The devastation of those years is likewise under the control of God as part of the expression of His anger at rebellious humanity (Psalm 7:11-16) which will then be fully ripe. By the same token, the earth and its inhabitants will be ripe for judgment (Revelation 14:15-20).

Before the start of the Tribulation, environmentally the earth will be tolerable as a whole, notwithstanding various environmental issues. There is now reasonably pure water, fertile soil, a livable temperature range and beneficial sea life such as fish. Fruit plants and trees nourish us. During the course of those 7 years, all of the rivers (and, I think, all of the surface lakes also) will become blood and unfit to drink. The first stage appears to be that one-third of the water will be unusable (Revelation 8:7-12) and thereafter the rest of the surface water will be taken away by God also (Revelation 16:3-4). I must assume that groundwater will remain drinkable or else all humanity would die within 2 weeks. All the life in the salt water will die also. This will eliminate navies and also tuna, salmon and many other beneficial fish from the human diet.

Because the green grass is burnt, it will not matter whether or not the soil is fertile. Cattle will die in massive numbers. Crops will be frozen or heated to death by the wild temperature swings that accompany the partial darkness (Revelation 8:12) followed by the scorching sun (Revelation 16:8-9—one might argue that the heat comes first, but I think that is less likely given the general principle that the birthpangs become more intense as one gets closer to the actual return of the Lord. In either case the temperature swings will play havoc with whatever agriculture is left.) Both food and water will be gravely short, which certainly matches up with the overview of Revelation 6.

Although I do not see direct references in Revelation other than the pale horse in Revelation 6, our Lord Jesus in Matthew 24 warned of pestilences—epidemics—that would come in the last days. One can certainly imagine that production and distribution of antibiotics and vaccines will be disrupted during these days. It is possible that someone will wage biological warfare. Even within military services disease is sometimes a greater killer than battle deaths. Sanitation will likewise decline under such conditions in both military and civilian life. God may also impose additional diseases upon rebellious humanity. In this connection, we should remember that human AIDS was unknown until about 1980. Sickness will contribute to starvation by making it impossible for key people to work and for the laborer to earn his wage. Near-starvation likewise will make people more prone to fatal diseases. Battle injuries will also open the door to fatal diseases.

Overall, it appears that one-half of the human race will die during these 7 years and that the rest will be about to die when Jesus Christ intervenes in person. In Revelation 6:8 one-fourth of the human race has died from the effects of the Four Horsemen to that point. Then in Revelation 9:15 there is associated with the drying of the Euphrates River the death of one-third of the remainder of the human race. I would assume that this stems from the great battle there and its consequences leading on to Armageddon. Since this one-third is probably calculated on the three-fourths of the original inhabitants which appear to remain alive to that point, the loss of life here is a second one-fourth of the original whole. No wonder that our Lord Jesus warned, *"Except those days should be shortened, no flesh should be saved. But for the elect's sake those days shall be shortened."* Matthew 24:22. So the human race will not go extinct after all.

My estimate of 50% loss of population because of God's judgments dovetails with the words of our Lord Jesus in Matthew 24:40-41, both of which record that He said, *"One shall be taken and the other left."* I have not understood that our Lord spoke with mathematical precision but rather in a general sense that one would die and another survive. But perhaps He was being more precise than I have realized. In the same vein He also in the Parable of the Ten Virgins divided them into five wise and five foolish. I do not view these passages as requiring an exact even division between those who survive the Tribulation and those who die, but there is the possibility that our Lord was truly being precise in the mathematical sense.

As to sequence, we can see clearly that these 7 terrible years (less an undetermined period by which they are cut short) start with an evil conqueror in Revelation 6:2 and end with Jesus Christ as the Conqueror in Revelation 19:11-21. Given the total results of the sway of the Anti-Christ, the precise order of events is of less importance than a basic grasp of the awful consequences of the comparative absence of God while the Anti-Christ is running his course. The consequences of the rule of the Man of Sin is a greatly magnified picture of the consequences of unconfessed and unforsaken sin in our own lives. Sin kills an individual life, a nation or an entire world. *"Sin, when it is finished, brings forth death."* James 1:15.

Revelation 6 spans the entire 7 years, starting with the Man of Sin as the rider on the white horse and ending with unrepentant humanity screaming and seeking in vain for a place to hide from the returning Jesus Christ. If we view Revelation 6 as a backbone of the description of the 7 years, it is relatively easy to see that the conquest of the Man of Sin, posing as a peacemaker (compare Daniel 9:24 where the Man of Sin seems to make a pact with Israel) in fact brings war in its wake. That would be typical of a man of Satan. War in turn brings famine and death, with epidemics contributing to deaths from both causes. It is probable that we should try to fit the trumpet judgments of Revelation 8 and the following chapters and the bowl judgments of Revelation 16 within this general framework in Revelation 6. I believe that the judgments within each series are in chronological order although they may overlap. However, each cycle of judgment describes the same 7 years or some portion of the 7 years, so that the three cycles should be superimposed on one another in some fashion rather than have each cycle of 7 in sequence after a previous completed cycle of 7 judgments.

If one is going to tie in Daniel 9:24-27 to Revelation, the beginning of the false covenant by the Anti-Christ mentioned in verse 24 is probably the beginning of the 7 years and the killing of the 2 witnesses in Revelation 11 (starting the very worst of the persecution) is probably linked to the breaking of the covenant 3½ years later. At that time I would likewise expect the Man of Sin to throw off his mask and demand worship as described in 2 Thessalonians 2. **But it is less important to try to know the precise timing of God's judgments than it is to fear Him now and commit to honor Him forever no matter what our friends, our family or humanity as a whole may do. We must by grace alone through faith alone with no claim of merit of our own worship and obey the true Messiah (or Christ), Jesus of Nazareth, as God in resurrected human flesh, equally with His Father and with the Holy Spirit. If we grasp that essential, the rest will in the end fall into place despite our fallibility.**

I have no means to make any precise fit of the four trumpet judgments of Revelation 8 within portions of Revelation 6. However, the fact that there is only one-third destruction probably places these first four judgments somewhere within the first half of the 7 years total. This impression is confirmed in Revelation 11:3, where God 2 true witnesses serve Him for a total of 1260 days, which comes to 42 months. The judgments inflicted by these witnesses are consistent with (not necessarily identical with) these preliminary judgments.

In broad overview, I view Revelation 12 as a very short-term prophecy of the rescue of the Christian church in Judea from the disaster to befall Judah and Jerusalem and secondarily as a picture of the survival of a remnant of the Church to the coming of Christ. I would view Revelation 13 as primarily a picture of the end-time worldwide persecution with aspects that also apply to the persecution under Nero (the original and lesser 666) which was to come right after Revelation was given originally to John. The persecution by Nero is a foreshadowing of the persecution by the Anti-Christ to come. Likewise, the destruction of Jerusalem and Israel in Matthew 24 is a foreshadowing of the destruction of the earth yet to come.

The bowls (or vials) of Revelation 16 seem to start later within the 7-year period, because the image of the Beast is already present in Revelation 16:2. I should also remark that the boils in Revelation 16:2 sounds like what Job suffered at the hands of Satan—but Job was healed by God and the followers of Satan will not be healed at all, not ever. Perhaps they are also like the boils that the Egyptians had when Pharaoh tried to hang on to the Israelites in Exodus 9:9-11. This time there is no relenting by God of the judgment.

The same basic comment about the parallel between the judgments on Egypt and on the world at the end applies to the waters becoming blood (Exodus 7:17-21) and the darkness (Exodus 10:22-23) imposed on the realm of the Beast. In Revelation 16:21 there is again the great hail which was probably similar to the hail upon Egypt in Exodus 9:18-25. I suspect that the hailstones in Revelation will be larger than those of the Exodus.

Even the death of the firstborn in Egypt can be a precedent for death of 50% of the population of the earth during the Tribulation.

One will note that all three cycles of Revelation end with an earthquake of unprecedented force. As I have written previously, I believe that this earthquake is the same one prophesied in Haggai 2:6-7 and in Isaiah 24:17-21 (and possibly the entire chapter). I further posit that each cycle in Revelation ends with the same earthquake, since the characteristics seem the same. This is not the earthquake that affects Jerusalem alone in Revelation 11:13. I think that the earthquakes of Revelation 6:14, of Revelation 8:5 (again a summary of the trumpets before they are spelled out), Revelation 11:19 and of Revelation 16:19-20 are one and the same with one another and with the great quake prophesied in Haggai and Isaiah. So the beginning points of the three cycles may differ (I think that Revelation 6 starts at the beginning of the Tribulation whereas the other 2 cycles probably start later and are more intense because they come to completion faster, with the bowl judgments starting the latest of the cycles and coming hardest and fastest) but the end points are simultaneous. One might visualize the three cycles as somewhat like a folk dance that starts relatively slowly and ends in a whirl that makes one dizzy. An example from classical music is the "Russian Sailors' Dance" by Glière. Ravel achieved a somewhat similar effect in "Bolero" by instrumentation and dynamics without varying tempo. Suffice it to say that humanity in the face of divine "shock and awe" is totally helpless.

We have discussed briefly the damage done to earth during the 7 years of the career of the Anti-Christ. The Bible also speaks of the clean-up when the Lord Jesus returns to stop the carnage. In Revelation 19:17-18 there is a summons to birds of carrion from all over the world to come and clean up the bodies of the armies that had been attacking Jerusalem and Israel. Their war plans had been stopped dead by the words of the Lord Jesus upon His return to earth. The bodies would be impossible to bury quickly and would constitute a terrible health hazard. The Lord's answer is the summons to the carrion birds to eat their fill and start cleaning up the awful mess. But this alone would not be enough. Ezekiel 39 not only mentions the vast numbers of birds but also a gigantic burial detail. People will find employment either marking the locations of bones and bodies or burying them and recycling their war equipment. So Isaiah 2:4 and Micah 4:3 will be fulfilled: *"They shall beat their swords into plowshares and their spears into pruning hooks."* While not every single step of a massive environmental clean-up is stated in Scripture, the outline is there. There is enough information to be assured that Jesus Christ will clean up the mess.

As horrible as life was under the Anti-Christ, it will be blessed under the direct rule of the genuine Jesus Christ. Some expositors believe that we will go directly from the rule of the Anti-Christ to heaven, where others believe based on Revelation 20 that there will be a 1000-year interval known as the Millenium where life will be maximized on this earth before the new creation of the new heavens and a new earth, both of which are perfect. Before we discuss that detail, the main point is the stark contrast between conditions under the Anti-Christ (being filled with the Devil) and under Jesus Christ, God and man combined in one person. We can perceive the contrast ahead of time from the prophetic Scriptures, but those who will survive the Tribulation would experience the vast difference. That difference is the precursor to the difference between the Lake of Fire and heaven.

It makes sense to contrast the rule of the Anti-Christ with the rule of Jesus Christ. These contrasts reflect the contrasting characters of Satan and of God. With God in the Garden there was life and love. Adam and Eve had fellowship with God every day. Satan introduced sin, conflict and death. When the Anti-Christ holds sway there will be famine. Under Jesus Christ agriculture will be bountiful (Amos 9:13-15). The Anti-Christ is a man of war; Jesus Christ is the Prince of Peace. The Anti-Christ is a liar; Jesus Christ is the walking Truth. The Anti-Christ is lawless; Jesus Christ will fulfill the prophecy to *"come and let us go up to the mountain of the Lord, to the house of the God of Jacob. And He will teach us of His ways, and we will walk in His paths, for out of Zion will go forth the Law, and the Word of the Lord from Jerusalem."* Isaiah 2:3. I would understand the "Word of the Lord" to refer both to the principles of God's Word but even more to God's walking, breathing and living Word, the Lord Jesus Christ. *"In the beginning was the Word, and the Word was with God, and the Word was God."* John 1:1.

WHERE DOES THE
RAPTURE FIT?

The word rapture comes from the Latin word meaning to snatch, as a person with a special harness might be snatched from the earth into a helicoptor or airplane. In English it has a useful association with great joy. With the Rapture will come great joy when God lifts His people from the earth to the air as He did Enoch, Elijah and the Lord Jesus Himself.

There are contrasting views of where the Rapture fits into the time sequence of God's judgments. The issue is not as to the <u>fact</u> of the Rapture. This is promised plainly in 1 Thessalonians 4:15-17. If we do not pass through death first, we will "meet the Lord in the air." But when in relation to the judgments of God? Because we are saved God has promised us deliverance from His vengeance. Jesus Christ has paid the full price for all of our sins. But are we promised a complete escape from persecution before He returns in His resurrection body to the earth? In terms of eternity the 7 years of the Tribulation are a blink of an eye, but because we are close but not yet in eternity (perhaps in the foothills now for all we know) the Tribulation looks like a towering mountain overshadowing us. So there is a strong tendency to want to escape all of the Tribulation (and all tribulation generally). Is the commonly taught doctrine that the Church will escape all of the Tribulation wishful thinking?

From a pastoral perspective, we need to be careful of our doctrine lest we produce hothouse Christians who cannot endure the real world.

In terms of the Parable of the Sower in Matthew 13, there is a real danger of producing either stony or thorny ground ostensible believers instead of firmly rooted, genuine, fruit-bearing Christians if we teach a Gospel that immediately delivers us from all earthly troubles before heaven.

I recognize that godly and good expositors will take issue with me, but I believe that the Church is raptured after the mid-point of the Tribulation. We cannot specify a precise time; the Lord Jesus stated that only the Father in heaven knew the exact time. Matthew 24:36. But the Apostle Paul did warn generally that *"through much tribulation we must enter the kingdom of God."* Acts 14:22. According to Strong's Concordance (generally accepted as the best Greek-English dictionary), the Greek word for "much" can also be and sometimes is translated as "great." If that reading were accepted, then Paul's preaching would be a strong hint at least that his converts might face the Tribulation or even some of the second half of the Tribulation, often called the Great Tribulation. In addition, Paul clearly stated the possibility that some of his original readers of 1 Thessalonians 4:15 would live to the Coming of the Lord *(then we who are alive and remain to the Coming of the Lord shall not precede those who have fallen asleep . . .").* I am sure that none of the members of that church in fact lived that long, but it was doctrinally possible. In addition, I view Revelation 11 and 13 as part of the same vision of the judgment of God and therefore view the killing of the two witnesses in Revelation 11 as the kick-off of the *pogrom* against Christians in the Last Days described in Revelation 13 and foreshadowed by the persecution under Nero. What Nero did in miniature the Anti-Christ will do in his whole domain, and even political rivals who contend against the Anti-Christ will be similar to him in regard to persecuting Christians and hating Israel. If God permits (unlike the case of the Lord Jesus where He had to accept the cup of suffering and did so to be the ransom for many), I would find it easier to by-pass tribulation generally and the Last Days in particular. But He as the Sovereign has every right to require me to go through part or all of it, to either receive a martyr's death or to escape death. Paul regarded suffering for Christ's sake as a gift (Philippians 1:29). Our Lord Jesus said that *"Blessed [or happy] are they who are persecuted for righteousness' sake, for theirs is the kingdom of heaven. Rejoice and be exceedingly glad, for so they persecuted the prophets that were before you."* Matthew 5:11-12. I do not feel this way now even though I know it is right, but God will supply this grace if and when it is necessary (compare Luke 21:14-15). But we must be willing and ready to suffer if it is truly necessary for the sake of the Lord Jesus or for the sake of what God has said is right. I see no reason in Scripture why I should expect conditions for the last generations of Christians should be fundamentally different than for the Apostles and their generation. And so I do not believe that the Rapture will be timed to spare all Christians from all of the Tribulation, although I do know that God has the power to spare Christians from particular tribulations as well as from divine wrath in general. (See Isaiah 26:20-21, set in the context of the Last Days, as one example.) I know also that some Christians will survive on earth to the Rapture (Mark 13:27). In the meantime, let us all study the Scriptures, thank God for His promises, and follow Matthew 6:33-34: *"But seek first the kingdom of God and His righteousness, and all of these things will be added to you. Therefore take no thought for tomorrow, for tomorrow will take thought for the things of itself. Sufficient for the day is its own evil."*

WHERE DOES THE SALVATION OF ISRAEL FIT?

While I cannot think of a direct verse that states directly that the final salvation of Israel is practically simultaneous with the Second Coming, I think that this can be pieced together. I would not make a great issue of the issue of precise timing so long as one believes the promises of God. I have earlier explained why I believe that Romans 11:26 means what it says that every person then living who is of national Israel shall be saved. [*Fight to the Finish,* Trafford Publishing Co. 2012, pp. 81ff., especially starting at p. 86] But Romans 11:26-7 if read naturally also tells us of sequence. *"There shall come out of Zion the Deliverer, and shall turn away ungodliness from Jacob, when I take away their sins."* Hebrews 12:22 uses Zion to refer to the heavenly Jerusalem, and that usage fits Romans 11 as well. So the passage is saying that the Deliverer shall come from the heavenly Jerusalem and deliver Jacob from its sins. And I must read "Jacob" as national Israel and not the Church for at least two reasons: (1) The Church will have been raptured as the Lord is descending into our atmosphere before He touches down on earth *("we . . . meet Him in the clouds"*—1 Thessalonians 4:17), and thus will no longer need deliverance; and (2) The usage of the fleshly name "Jacob" indicates a sinful nation instead of a sanctified church sometimes referred to as "Israel" (for example Galatians 6:16 and compare Romans 2:29, Romans 4:16 and really all of Romans 4, and 1 Peter 2:9—'a holy nation'—where the Church is referred to in terms originally applicable to the nation of Israel). The nation to be delivered eventually was as Paul wrote an enemy of the Gospel (11:28), which applies to national Israel but not to the Church. So we should read verse 26 as teaching that the Lord Jesus will return to earth to save "Jacob"—national Israel in the flesh. This fits with the Lord killing the hostile armies at Armageddon with but a word from His mouth on His return. Revelation 19:21. That in turn places the salvation of Israel shortly after the salvation of the last Gentile (*"the fulness of the Gentiles has come in"*—Romans 11:25, compare Revelation 6:9-11 for the concept of a number pre-determined by God). This will also be virtually simultaneous with the resurrection of the dead (or at least the martyred dead depending on one's view of Revelation 20), which in turn comes just before the Rapture of believers (1 Thessalonians 4:16-17). So all of these events are clustered together very close to the end of the Tribulation and the slaughter of the world's armies as portrayed in Revelation 19.

Isaiah 65-66 appears to confirm this reading of Romans 11 and of its integration into Revelation. If one reads Isaiah 65, one will note parallels with the observation in Romans 11 that most Jews of Paul's generation were rejected in favor of Gentiles (especially Isaiah 65:1-7). Then the following verses teach about the remnant that is spared God's judgment and saved. Once again this is found in Romans 11. Then there are promises of bliss and blessing forever; reasonable people can differ whether these promises are fulfilled solely in the new heavens and the new earth of verse 17 or whether they will be initially fulfilled during the Millenium and then finally fulfilled totally in the new heavens and the new earth. I come down on the side of those who believe in a Millenium on earth before the new heavens and the new earth as I read Revelation 20 and the prophecies of Isaiah found in Isaiah 2, 4, 11, 35, and in other places, but this is a detail and not a central issue of faith.

Then we come to Isaiah 66, which stresses the suddenness of the change in the descendants of Jacob from unbelieving traitors against God to a holy people for God (especially verses 7-8). This again matches up with Romans 11:26-29. In thought Isaiah 66:4 (*"I will choose their delusions . . .*") matches up with 2 Thessalonians 2:11 (*"God will send them strong delusion . . ."*). Then both Isaiah 66:12-14 and Zechariah 12:10-12 and 14:5 tie in with the deliverance of Jerusalem referred to in Romans 11:26-32 and especially with Revelation 16:19 (the division of the city contrasts with the total fall of all Gentile cities). Certainly the theme of the vengeance of God against His enemies in Isaiah 66 matches with Romans 9 and 11 and also with Revelation 19. Likewise the comfort of God matches with the comfort given in the beginning of Revelation 19 and in chapters 21-22. Isaiah 66 ends similarly to Revelation with its clear contrast between the joy of those made righteous by God and the torments of the wicked. One way to get an introduction to Revelation is to read Isaiah 65-66 first, just as Isaiah 24-27 also summarizes the judgment of God as unveiled in more detail in Revelation.

A BRIEF SKETCH OF THE TRIAL PORTRAYED IN MATTHEW 25:31-46

When one reads this section of Scripture, the similarities to a human trial are striking. This is not a single trial but separate trials of many defendants in the presence of all. In this way this is like a busy, crowded traffic court, although the consequences are infinitely greater. Matthew 25:32 indicates that all the nations are present; Revelation 20:12 states that the famous and the unknown, the mighty and the lowly alike shall be there. No human being will be missing, regardless of how or when one's body perished. To the extent that any bailiffs are needed, the holy angels will be there in ample power and numbers. People will be separated into two divisions, symbolized as sheep (meek followers) and goats (stubborn). But what will be so noteworthy will be the appearance of the Judge. We know from John 5 that He is Jesus Christ, the Son of God. But his appearance in Revelation 1 is so striking that He will make this unlike any human court that has ever sat in judgment. According to that chapter, the Lord is clothed in white (rather than the traditional black in most human courts) with a gold sash on His chest. His voice has the power of a waterfall. His hair is white like wool, corresponding to the title of Ancient of Days in Daniel 7:9 (Daniel's portrayal of the Judgment is in Daniel 7:9-14). He judges from a fiery throne rather than from a raised dais to which we are accustomed. He has "fire in His eyes" and His feet shine as brass. This appearance of the Lord Jesus will strike pure terror into all the "goats" in the courtroom, probably surpassing even the terror of Revelation 6:19-20. In both Daniel and Revelation books are opened for purposes of judgment. If one's sins are not blotted out by the blood of Jesus Christ, seeing that book opened must be a moment of dread that cannot be described from anything we know on earth.

In addition to the overwhelming appearance of the Son of God, there is also the throne from which He judges, described in Revelation 4:2-7. For believers, there will be the comforting sight of the emerald rainbow, reminding them of the promise that God made to Noah that He would not flood the entire earth again. For unbelievers, the voices, thunders and lightnings from the throne itself will be indications of God's anger which is about to be unleashed on them. This will be "shock and awe" in Biblical proportions. Although angels are available, I would suggest that no bailiffs will actually be necessary. The throne's appearance and especially the appearance of Jesus Christ as the Ancient of Days as the Judge will together be more than ample to keep order. I really do not know just how we will react. I know that the Apostle John fell down as if dead when he saw the risen Jesus. (Revelation 1:17) Even before His death and resurrection, the soldiers sent to arrest the Lord Jesus could not stand in the face of a tiny bit of His power. (John 18:6) Philippians 2:10-11 prophesies that *"Every knee shall bow . . . and every tongue confess that Jesus Christ is Lord, to the glory of God the Father."* In a human court the people stand in respect for the judge or at least for his office when the judge enters. People will not stand when the Lord Jesus takes His judgment throne. My question is whether they will stop at kneeling or whether they will fall all the way to prone on the floor with faces to the ground. But I am positive that nobody will be able to offer the least resistance to His justice.

Let me try to imagine the hearing of one relatively infamous man: Joseph Stalin. It is true that many of his actions were worse than those of most people and that he was responsible for many more deaths than most. But still there are enough parallels between the attitudes of Stalin with modern attitudes that we should indeed be afraid to face Jesus Christ without His forgiveness in advance.

One of the entries in the book would show that Stalin was taught as a child that Jesus Christ was the Son of God. Stalin turned away from this truth for atheism and likewise cast off the Ten Commandments for a lifetime of revolutionary activity that started with bank robbery (stealing) and climaxed in murder and genocide during the 1930s. Special targets were Ukrainians, intellectuals, military officers, religious leaders and believers and even Communists who were thought to be insufficiently subservient to the Cult of Personality (Khrushchev's telling phrase from his Secret Speech in 1956) that Stalin created around himself. This was pride on top of Stalin's unbelief. Needless to say, Stalin did not want the presence of God near him. The outward consequences of the unbelief and pride included the slow mass murder of millions in the *gulag*. Stalin was also cruel to his wife and friends, at least contributing to their deaths. Stalin had his henchmen seize Bibles wherever they could to keep the Word of God from the people. Stalin's planned campaign against the Jews was cut short by his death from a stroke. And these are only some of the known highlights of Stalin's sins.

It is unlikely that you personally have participated in murder as did Stalin, but what about your unbelief and your pride? What about your disregard for the Bible? If you have a family, do you teach the Bible to your children and other members of the family? How kind are you within your family? For many of my readers, I am afraid that an honest examination would find the same root attitudes in you that were in Stalin, admittedly to a lesser degree. But is it any real comfort if you have stage 3 metastatic cancer that someone else has a more advanced stage 4 cancer? Can you find any real comfort that your degree of sin is less than that of Stalin?

I have stressed unbelief as a root sin from which many other sins spring. In fact you cannot even begin to please God without saving faith. Hebrews 11:6 says plainly that *"Without faith it is impossible to please Him. He that comes to God must believe that He is* [that is, believe in His existence] *and that He is a rewarder of those who diligently seek Him."* If you are hoping to offset your sin with good things you have done, that won't work. On this general subject Ezekiel 18 is a detailed account. It warns that *"the soul that sins shall die."* Ezekiel 18:20. And James tells us that if we violate even one principle of the Law, that we are guilty before the Law as having violated them all. James 2:10. And Ezekiel warns that when a righteous man (apparently righteous, generally righteous or relatively righteous) violates the Law, then all of his righteousness will not even count—that man will die for his sin. Ezekiel 18:26. There is no offset in God's judgments. You are either viewed as the sinner you are (*"All have sinned and come short of the glory of God."*—Romans 3:23 and see also 1 Kings 8:46 which agrees) or through faith in the saving sacrifice of Jesus Christ you are viewed and treated as perfectly righteous despite your actual sins, which have been forgiven. There is no middle ground of guilt of a lesser offense such as we sometimes find in human courts. Before God you are either guilty or innocent, and you will be either taken to heaven or cast into the Lake of Fire. And this judgment is forever and ever.

If sin and unbelief are the ruling principles in your life, you are in danger of hearing those terrible words from Jesus Christ in His voice with the power of a waterfall, *"Depart from Me, you cursed, into everlasting fire prepared for the Devil and his angels."* Matthew 25:41. And indeed the angels will carry out the divine sentence without delay and without appeal.

Obviously the judgment is totally different for the genuine believer in Jesus Christ. Let me take Saul of Tarsus, later known as the Apostle Paul, as an example. We know from Acts 6 and 7 that Paul was a willing accomplice in the murder of Stephen, one of the original deacons. Paul confesses himself to have been the chief of sinners in 1 Timothy 1:15. When the case of Saul of Tarsus is called, what happens? His name is found to be written in the Book of Life (Revelation 20:12, 21:27; Philippians 4:3). When the books are examined for the sins of Saul of Tarsus, nothing is found! One might find an entry something like this: EXPUNGED BY THE BLOOD OF THE LAMB (Acts 3:19). Not only so, but the Law by which Saul of Tarsus is to be judged will not be found either. On the Cross, Jesus Christ was *"blotting out the handwriting of the ordinances which was against us . . ."* Colossians 2:14. *"Where there is no law there is no transgression."* Romans 4:15. So Paul goes free to heaven with his rewards.

In Virginia Federal courts and on the appellate bench, after the hearing is concluded the judges have a tradition of coming off the bench and shaking hands with the lawyers and even with the defendant. From the standpoint of the lawyer, this is a good reminder of the fundamental equality of all people. I do not know whether Jesus Christ will come off His throne then and there to embrace His child whom He has acquitted and pardoned then and there or will wait until later, but we will be embraced then by the Judge, Who is our spiritual brother (Romans 8:29) as well as our Lord and Judge. We will hear in His full voice His verdict, *"Well done, good and faithful servant."* (Matthew 25:21-23) If receiving a diploma is meaningful now, just try to imagine the joy of hearing that word spoken by the Judge of all in the presence of witnesses too many to count.

Regardless of the precise order of events, the believer is triply safe because: (1) His or her sins have been blotted out; (2) The Law itself will be blotted out for him or her; and (3) His or her brother and Advocate (1 John 2:1), Who has already died to save that person, has the power of final judgment. Hallelujah!